IN ASSOCIATION WITH

✕ SQA

HODDER
GIBSON
Model Papers
WITH ANSWERS

PLUS: Official SQA Specimen Paper & 2015 Past Paper With Answers

Higher for CfE
Graphic Communication

2014 Specimen Question Paper, Model Papers & 2015 Exam

HODDER
GIBSON
AN HACHETTE UK COMPANY

This book contains the official 2014 SQA Specimen Question Paper and 2015 Exam for Higher for CfE Graphic Communication, with associated SQA approved answers modified from the official marking instructions that accompany the paper.

In addition the book contains model papers, together with answers, plus study skills advice. These papers, some of which may include a limited number of previously published SQA questions, have been specially commissioned by Hodder Gibson, and have been written by experienced senior teachers and examiners in line with the new Higher for CfE syllabus and assessment outlines, Spring 2014. This is not SQA material but has been devised to provide further practice for Higher for CfE examinations in 2015 and beyond.

Hodder Gibson is grateful to the copyright holders, as credited on the final page of the Answer Section, for permission to use their material. Every effort has been made to trace the copyright holders and to obtain their permission for the use of copyright material. Hodder Gibson will be happy to receive information allowing us to rectify any error or omission in future editions.

Hachette UK's policy is to use papers that are natural, renewable and recyclable products and made from wood grown in sustainable forests. The logging and manufacturing processes are expected to conform to the environmental regulations of the country of origin.

Orders: please contact Bookpoint Ltd, 130 Park Drive, Milton Park, Abingdon, Oxon OX14 4SE. Telephone: (44) 01235 827720. Fax: (44) 01235 400454. Lines are open 9.00–5.00, Monday to Saturday, with a 24-hour message answering service. Visit our website at www.hoddereducation.co.uk. Hodder Gibson can be contacted direct on: Tel: 0141 848 1609; Fax: 0141 889 6315; email: hoddergibson@hodder.co.uk

This collection first published in 2015 by
Hodder Gibson, an imprint of Hodder Education,
An Hachette UK Company
2a Christie Street
Paisley PA1 1NB

Typeset by Aptara, Inc.

Printed in the UK

A catalogue record for this title is available from the British Library

ISBN: 978-1-4718-6077-5

3 2 1

2016 2015

Introduction

Study Skills – what you need to know to pass exams!

Pause for thought

Many students might skip quickly through a page like this. After all, we all know how to revise. Do you really though?

Think about this:

"IF YOU ALWAYS DO WHAT YOU ALWAYS DO, YOU WILL ALWAYS GET WHAT YOU HAVE ALWAYS GOT."

Do you like the grades you get? Do you want to do better? If you get full marks in your assessment, then that's great! Change nothing! This section is just to help you get that little bit better than you already are.

There are two main parts to the advice on offer here. The first part highlights fairly obvious things which are also very important. The second part makes suggestions about revision that you might not have thought about but which WILL help you.

Part 1

DOH! It's so obvious but …

Start revising in good time

Don't leave it until the last minute   this will make you panic.

Make a revision timetable that sets out work time AND play time.

Sleep and eat!

Obvious really, and very helpful. Avoid arguments or stressful things too – even games that wind you up. You need to be fit, awake and focused!

Know your place!

Make sure you know exactly WHEN and WHERE your exams are.

Know your enemy!

Make sure you know what to expect in the exam.

How is the paper structured?

How much time is there for each question?

What types of question are involved?

Which topics seem to come up time and time again?

Which topics are your strongest and which are your weakest?

Are all topics compulsory or are there choices?

Learn by DOING!

There is no substitute for past papers and practice papers – they are simply essential! Tackling this collection of papers and answers is exactly the right thing to be doing as your exams approach.

Part 2

People learn in different ways. Some like low light, some bright. Some like early morning, some like evening / night. Some prefer warm, some prefer cold. But everyone uses their BRAIN and the brain works when it is active. Passive learning – sitting gazing at notes – is the most INEFFICIENT way to learn anything. Below you will find tips and ideas for making your revision more effective and maybe even more enjoyable. What follows gets your brain active, and active learning works!

Activity 1 – Stop and review

Step 1

When you have done no more than 5 minutes of revision reading STOP!

Step 2

Write a heading in your own words which sums up the topic you have been revising.

Step 3

Write a summary of what you have revised in no more than two sentences. Don't fool yourself by saying, 'I know it but I cannot put it into words'. That just means you don't know it well enough. If you cannot write your summary, revise that section again, knowing that you must write a summary at the end of it. Many of you will have notebooks full of blue/black ink writing. Many of the pages will not be especially attractive or memorable so try to liven them up a bit with colour as you are reviewing and rewriting. **This is a great memory aid, and memory is the most important thing.**

Activity 2 – Use technology!

Why should everything be written down? Have you thought about 'mental' maps, diagrams, cartoons and colour to help you learn? And rather than write down notes, why not record your revision material?

What about having a text message revision session with friends? Keep in touch with them to find out how and what they are revising and share ideas and questions.

Why not make a video diary where you tell the camera what you are doing, what you think you have learned and what you still have to do? No one has to see or hear it but the process of having to organise your thoughts in a formal way to explain something is a very important learning practice.

Be sure to make use of electronic files. You could begin to summarise your class notes. Your typing might be slow but it will get faster and the typed notes will be easier to read than the scribbles in your class notes. Try to add different fonts and colours to make your work stand out. You can easily Google relevant pictures, cartoons and diagrams which you can copy and paste to make your work more attractive and MEMORABLE.

Activity 3 – This is it. Do this and you will know lots!

Step 1

In this task you must be very honest with yourself! Find the SQA syllabus for your subject (www.sqa.org.uk). Look at how it is broken down into main topics called MANDATORY knowledge. That means stuff you MUST know.

Step 2

BEFORE you do ANY revision on this topic, write a list of everything that you already know about the subject. It might be quite a long list but you only need to write it once. It shows you all the information that is already in your long-term memory so you know what parts you do not need to revise!

Step 3

Pick a chapter or section from your book or revision notes. Choose a fairly large section or a whole chapter to get the most out of this activity.

With a buddy, use Skype, Facetime, Twitter or any other communication you have, to play the game "If this is the answer, what is the question?". For example, if you are revising Geography and the answer you provide is "meander", your buddy would have to make up a question like "What is the word that describes a feature of a river where it flows slowly and bends often from side to side?".

Make up 10 "answers" based on the content of the chapter or section you are using. Give this to your buddy to solve while you solve theirs.

Step 4

Construct a wordsearch of at least 10 × 10 squares. You can make it as big as you like but keep it realistic. Work together with a group of friends. Many apps allow you to make wordsearch puzzles online. The words and phrases can go in any direction and phrases can be split. Your puzzle must only contain facts linked to the topic you are revising. Your task is to find 10 bits of information to hide in your puzzle but you must not repeat information that you used in Step 3. DO NOT show where the words are. Fill up empty squares with random letters. Remember to keep a note of where your answers are hidden but do not show your friends. When you have a complete puzzle, exchange it with a friend to solve each other's puzzle.

Step 5

Now make up 10 questions (not "answers" this time) based on the same chapter used in the previous two tasks. Again, you must find NEW information that you have not yet used. Now it's getting hard to find that new information! Again, give your questions to a friend to answer.

Step 6

As you have been doing the puzzles, your brain has been actively searching for new information. Now write a NEW LIST that contains only the new information you have discovered when doing the puzzles. Your new list is the one to look at repeatedly for short bursts over the next few days. Try to remember more and more of it without looking at it. After a few days, you should be able to add words from your second list to your first list as you increase the information in your long-term memory.

FINALLY! Be inspired...

Make a list of different revision ideas and beside each one write THINGS I HAVE tried, THINGS I WILL try and THINGS I MIGHT try. Don't be scared of trying something new.

And remember – FAIL TO PREPARE AND PREPARE TO FAIL!

Higher Graphic Communication

The course

The aims of the course are to enable you to understand how graphic communication is used every day in industry and society and to develop skills and techniques used in creating graphics to suit a range of functions and purposes.

The types of graphics you will learn about include:

- **Preliminary** design graphics
- Technical **production** drawings
- High impact **promotional** graphics.

These are known as the **3Ps**. Your coursework projects and exam questions are based on these types of graphics and the impact graphics have on society and the environment. The knowledge you need for the exam will come from the work you do during your project work in class.

How you are assessed and graded

The grade you achieve at the end of your course depends on a number of assessments.

Unit Assessment

Both Units (2D Graphics and 3D and Pictorial Graphics) are assessed on a pass or fail basis.

Both Units must be passed in order to qualify for a course award.

Course Assessment

The grade for the Higher course is derived from two course assessments:

- **The assignment**

This is the project you will complete towards the second half of your course and it is worth **70 marks**.

- **The exam paper**

The course exam paper is also worth **70 marks**.

The total, 140 marks, is graded from A to D for a pass.

The exam

The exam is **two hours** long and is worth a total of **70 marks**. It will include a mix of short questions and more extended questions relating to preliminary, production and promotional graphics. There will be different types of graphics to interpret and understand before questions can be answered. These graphics can be complex and detailed and it would be a mistake to jump straight in with answers. It is vital to spend time studying the graphics and the questions first.

Look at the marks awarded for each question. This is a good indicator of the length of answer you should give.

For example, a 3-mark question will need you to make three distinct points, while a 1-mark question may require only a single point. Each mark should take around 1 ½ minutes to earn with some reading time left over, so plan your time accordingly.

Sketching

Exam questions will be set so that you can answer in writing. However, some questions will invite you to answer using annotated sketches or drawings and space will be left so that you may sketch your answer. **Always take this opportunity.**

Remember:

- This is an exam about graphics and you have all the graphic skills you need.
- It is easier and quicker to describe your answer graphically with annotations.
- The quality of sketching will not be assessed but the clarity of your answer is important so make the sketches and annotations clear.
- Plan your sketches in a light pencil and firm in with a black pen.

Answering 3D CAD modelling questions

You should always:

- study the model and any other sketches, drawings or notes.
- identify what modelling techniques have been used (extrude, revolve, loft, helices or extrude along a path).
- describe the steps such as: new sketch, draw profile, select axis and revolve, etc.
- include reference to the dimensions provided.
- describe any additional edits used: array, subtract, shell, etc.
- and importantly, make sketches to help describe the steps.
- ensure your sketches are firmed in and outlined in pen to enable scanning of your answers.

Answering creative layout questions

These questions will ask you to identify how DTP features and design elements and principles have been used in a layout. You will always be asked to explain how the use of these features improves the layout. You should always:

- study the layout: don't rush this.
- identify the DTP features or elements and principles used.

- think carefully about how it improves the layout: does it add contrast, create harmony, suggest depth, develop a dominant focal point, unify the layout, create emphasis or connect or separate parts? The feature you are asked about will do one or more of these things. Your task is to spot which and explain how.

At the end of the exam, read over your answers and read the questions again. Double-check that you have answered the question. You should have plenty of time.

Skills and knowledge

The skills and knowledge the exam will test are:

Problem solving: explain how you would model, render or assemble a 3D CAD model or create a 2D CAD drawing.

Creative skills: describe how the graphic designer used design elements and principles to create an effective layout.

DTP features and edits: explain how the graphic designer used DTP features to achieve an effective layout.

Advantages and disadvantages: justify the best methods to choose when creating graphics.

Knowledge of drawing standards: explain how drawing standards should be applied to orthographic and pictorial drawings including technical detail.

Spatial awareness: testing your ability to interpret and understand drawings.

Graphics in society: explain how graphics are used in society.

Graphics and the environment: explain how we can create and use graphics without damaging our fragile environment.

Practising the type of questions you are likely to face in the Higher exam is vital. This book will give you experience of the problem solving and creative layout questions you will experience in the exam. Ensure you tackle these important sections before your prelim and course exams.

Good luck!

Remember that the rewards for passing Higher Graphic Communication are well worth it! Your pass will help you get the future you want for yourself. In the exam, be confident in your own ability. If you're not sure how to answer a question, trust your instincts and just give it a go anyway. Keep calm and don't panic! GOOD LUCK!

2014 Specimen
Question Paper

H

National Qualifications
SPECIMEN ONLY

Mark

SQ22/H/01

Graphic Communication

Date — Not applicable

Duration — 2 hours

Fill in these boxes and read what is printed below.

Full name of centre

Town

Forename(s)

Surname

Number of seat

Date of birth

Day   Month   Year

D D   M M   Y Y

Scottish candidate number

Total marks — 70

Attempt ALL questions.

Write your answers clearly in the spaces provided in this booklet. Additional space for answers is provided at the end of this booklet. If you use this space you must clearly identify the question number you are attempting.

All dimensions are in mm.

All technical sketches and drawings use third angle projection.

You may use rulers, compasses or trammels for measuring.

In all questions you may use sketches and annotations to support your answer if you wish.

Use **blue** or **black** ink.

Before leaving the examination room you must give this booklet to the Invigilator; if you do not, you may lose all the marks for this paper.

Attempt ALL questions

Total marks — 70

MARKS | DO NOT WRITE IN THIS MARGIN

1. A public building that was constructed in the 1950s is to be modernised. The original drawings were produced manually in paper format. The architect has requested that the manual drawings be converted to a digital format and sent electronically.

   The conversion methods being considered are: scanning the original drawings **or** reproducing the drawings using CAD software.

   (a)   (i)   Compare the two methods in terms of their suitability for this task.   **4**

MARKS

1. (a) (continued)

(ii) Explain two possible disadvantages that may be encountered when two different people or companies work together on the same project using CAD.

2

CAD simulation could be used to test aspects of the design of the building.

(b) Identify an aspect of the design that could be tested through a CAD simulation.

1

(c) Identify an advantage of a "paperless office" to an architectural business.

1

MARKS | DO NOT WRITE IN THIS MARGIN

2. The sketches below were used by a CAD technician to create a 3D model of a portable speaker casing. The 3D model will be used to make production drawings and a promotional illustration.

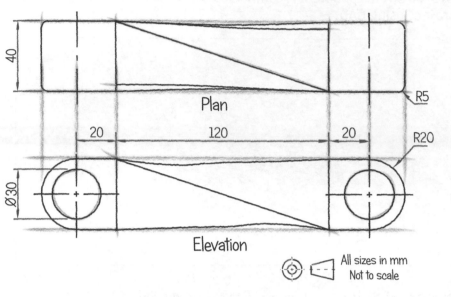

40

Plan

20   120   20

R5

Ø30

R20

Elevation

All sizes in mm
Not to scale

Orthographic sketch

The CAD technician sketched a modelling plan before creating the 3D model. The first two stages of the modelling plan are shown below.

(a) Describe the 3D modelling techniques proposed for each stage, making reference to all relevant dimensions from the orthographic sketch. You can sketch, annotate the sketches provided and/or use text in your answer.

(i)   2

(ii)   2

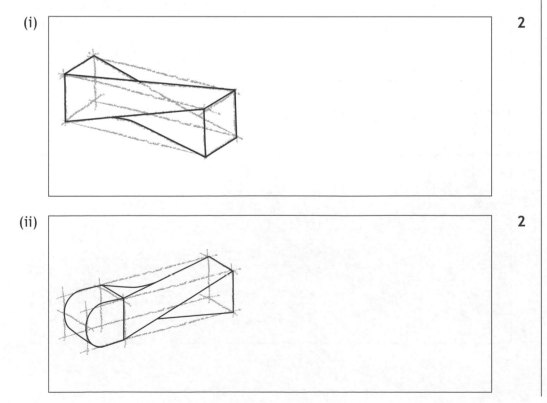

MARKS | DO NOT WRITE IN THIS MARGIN

2.   (continued)

Solid model of the
portable speaker casing

Component parts of the
portable speaker casing

A solid model of the portable speaker casing and the two components generated from it are shown above.

(b)   Describe, using a "top-down" approach, the techniques used to create the two component parts from the solid model.   You can sketch, annotate and/or use text in your answer.

4

MARKS | DO NOT WRITE IN THIS MARGIN

2. (continued)

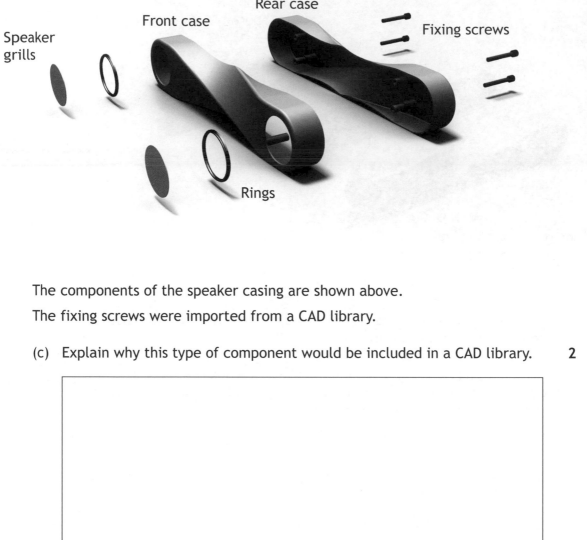

Speaker grills

Front case

Rear case

Fixing screws

Rings

The components of the speaker casing are shown above.

The fixing screws were imported from a CAD library.

(c) Explain why this type of component would be included in a CAD library. **2**

MARKS | DO NOT WRITE IN THIS MARGIN

2. (continued)

The two component parts of the portable speaker casing need to be assembled within the CAD software.

(d) Outline the 3D modelling techniques used to fully constrain the two component parts. You may use annotated sketches to support your answer if you wish.

2

2. (continued)

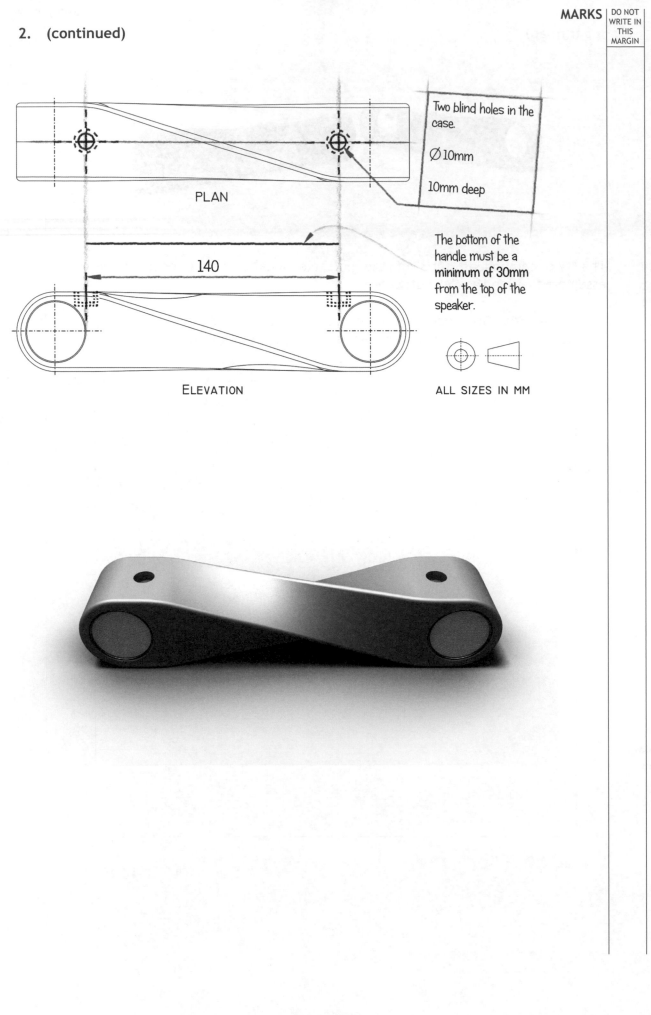

PLAN

140

ELEVATION

Two blind holes in the case.

Ø10mm

10mm deep

The bottom of the handle must be a minimum of 30mm from the top of the speaker.

ALL SIZES IN MM

MARKS

2. **(continued)**

The portable speaker casing design has been modified to allow a simple handle to be attached. These modifications have been sketched on the production drawings and shown on the 3D model on the left.

(e) Produce a modelling plan which could be used to create a 3D CAD model of a simple handle to fit the blind holes in the casing. The handle will be glued into the holes. You can sketch, annotate, and/or use text in your answer.

4

MARKS

3. The promotional layout below is used to attract consumers to a new product.

The BIO+ball is an innovative new product that helps to ensure the well being of you and your family.

Whilst the BIO+ball is innocently floating around in the kitchen sink it is constantly killing off harmful germs.

BIO+ball is so versatile that is can be used when cleaning dishes, preparing vegetables and when washing hands.

Explain how the graphic designer has used typeface, colour and choice of images to attract consumers.

4

MARKS | DO NOT WRITE IN THIS MARGIN

4. Components that make up a pulley wheel assembly are shown below as an exploded view.

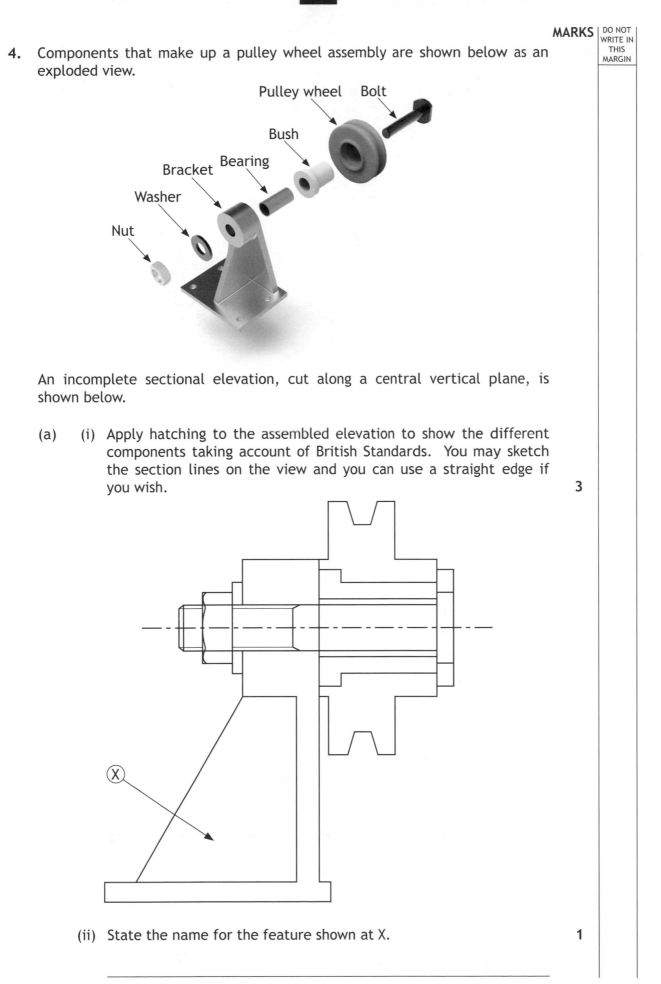

An incomplete sectional elevation, cut along a central vertical plane, is shown below.

(a) (i) Apply hatching to the assembled elevation to show the different components taking account of British Standards. You may sketch the section lines on the view and you can use a straight edge if you wish.

3

(ii) State the name for the feature shown at X.

1

_____

MARKS | DO NOT WRITE IN THIS MARGIN

4. (a) (continued)

The bolt used in the assembly has flat sections on the end for a spanner to fit.

(iii) Apply the British Standards convention for this flat on the bolt shown below (Figure 1).

1

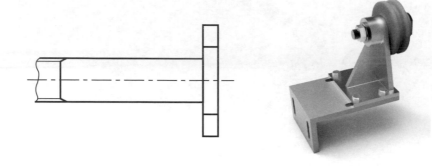

Figure 1   **Figure 2**

The 3D view in Figure 2 shows the pulley assembly bolted by the base to another component. The drawing below shows the three stages.

Stage 1 — a blind hole is machined in the component

Stage 2 — a thread is cut into the blind hole

Stage 3 — an M10 bolt and washer is fitted to secure the pulley assembly

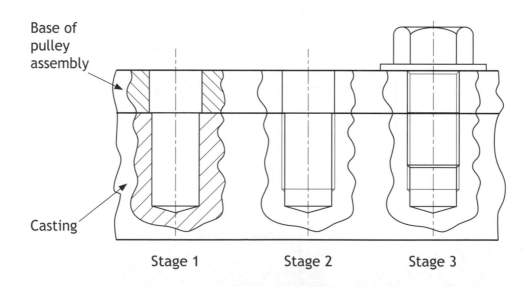

Base of pulley assembly

Casting

Stage 1   Stage 2   Stage 3

(b)   (i) Apply hatching to **Stage 2** and **Stage 3** above taking account of British Standards and conventions. You may sketch the section lines on the view and you can use a straight edge if you wish.

2

MARKS | DO NOT WRITE IN THIS MARGIN

4. (b) (continued)

(ii) Explain the term "blind hole" at Stage 1.

1

(iii) What does the "M" stand for on the M10 bolt?

1

(iv) Determine the depth of the hole for the thread cut at Stage 2.

1

(v) State the type of section shown at Stages 1 to 3.

1

The holes on the base of the pulley assembly are 10·5 mm with a tolerance of −0·15 and +0·15 applied.

(vi) Apply the dimensional tolerance to the hole in Stage 1 taking account of British Standards.

1

5. The elevation of two interpenetrating cylindrical pipes is shown below. A surface development of interpenetrating cylindrical pipes is being generated using 2D CAD. The elevation and part construction work is shown below.

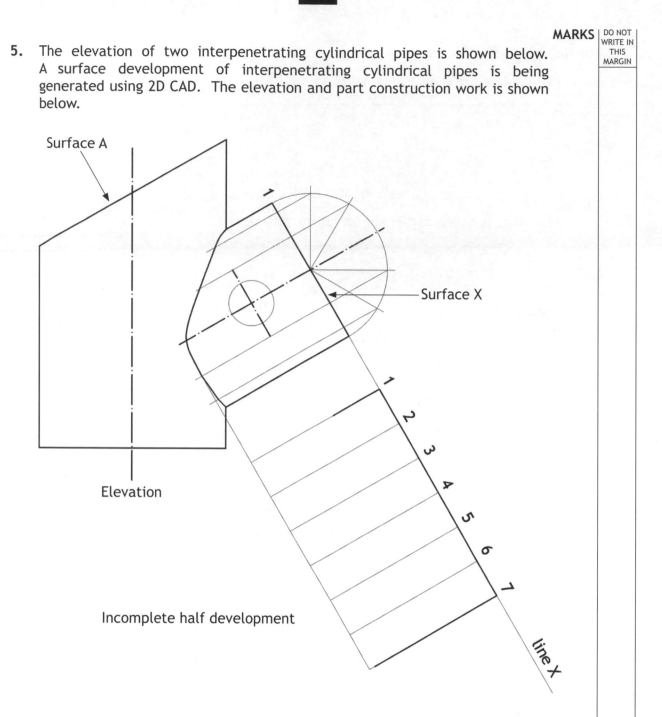

Surface A

Surface X

Elevation

Incomplete half development

line X

Line X has been drawn and will be offset to the left to create a series of parallel lines to locate the intersection for plotting the points.

MARKS | DO NOT WRITE IN THIS MARGIN

5. (continued)

(a) Complete the table provided indicating the offset required to locate the position of the points on each generator given (1—7) and the centre point for the circle.

2

Generator line	Offset from line X (mm)
1	
2	
3	
4	
5	
6	
7	
Circle centre point	

The true shape of surface A is shown below.

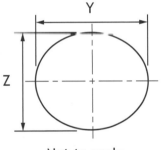

Not to scale

(b) What are the full dimensions for Y and Z on surface A?

1

Y = _____   Z = _____

MARKS | DO NOT WRITE IN THIS MARGIN

6. Use the three layouts in the **Question 6 supplement** provided to answer this question.

Three promotional layouts for "One Stop Kit Shop", a cycling accessories chain, are shown.

The layouts are aimed at three different target markets and will be displayed in three different magazines.

Target market layout 1: (45—65 years) male and female, leisure cycling, working and retired singles and couples, grown-up families, TV influences: gardening and travel shows

Target market layout 2: (25—45 years) male and female, working, keen cyclists, adventure cycling, young families or no family commitments, TV influences: sport and Top Gear

Target market layout 3: (15—25 years) predominantly male, serious adventure and mountain biking, single, independent, TV influences: reality shows, indie and grunge music

The graphic designer has used a range of design elements and principles in each of the three layouts to appeal to the different target markets.

(a) Explain why the styles of typeface used in layout 1 will appeal to its target market.   2

(b) Explain how the use of shape enhances layout 2.   2

MARKS | DO NOT WRITE IN THIS MARGIN

6. **(continued)**

In layout 2, three lines, two blue and one orange, are used.

(c) Explain how each of these lines improves layout 2. Each of your explanations should be different.

3

Advancing and receding colours have been used in each of the layouts.

(d) Select one of the layouts. Identify an advancing colour used in it, and describe the impact this colour has on the layout.

2

In layout _____ the advancing colour is _____.

The effect this colour has on the layout is:

Different forms of balance have been used in the layouts. In layout 1 the cyclists are placed off-centre, whilst in layout 2 the cyclist is placed in the centre of the layout.

(e) (i) Explain one challenge that placing a main item in the centre of a layout gives the graphic designer.

1

MARKS | DO NOT WRITE IN THIS MARGIN

6. (e) (continued)

(ii) Explain the benefit of placing a main item off-centre in a layout (other than your answer to 6(e)(i)).

1

(f) Explain three different ways in which the graphic designer has used design elements and principles in layout 3 to appeal to its target market.

3

MARKS | DO NOT WRITE IN THIS MARGIN

7. Use "The Colour and the Shape" articles (layout A and layout B) from the **Question 7 supplement** provided to answer this question.

A graphic designer has created a magazine double-page spread for a home furnishing publication as shown in layout A. After development, the graphic designer enhanced the layout and produced a pre-press copy, layout B.

(a) Explain **two** reasons for using **headers** and **footers** in a multi-page document.

2

(b) Examine the feature shown below.

(i) State the name of this feature which is in each corner of layout B.

1

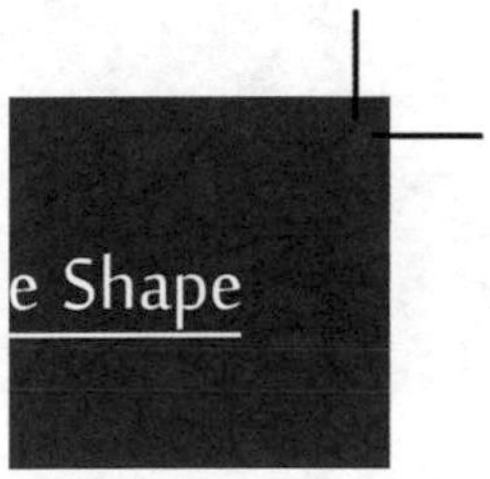

e Shape

(ii) Explain the purpose of this feature.

1

(iii) Explain why the graphic designer used bleed in layout B.

1

MARKS | DO NOT WRITE IN THIS MARGIN

7.   (continued)

Examine the layering tree shown below.

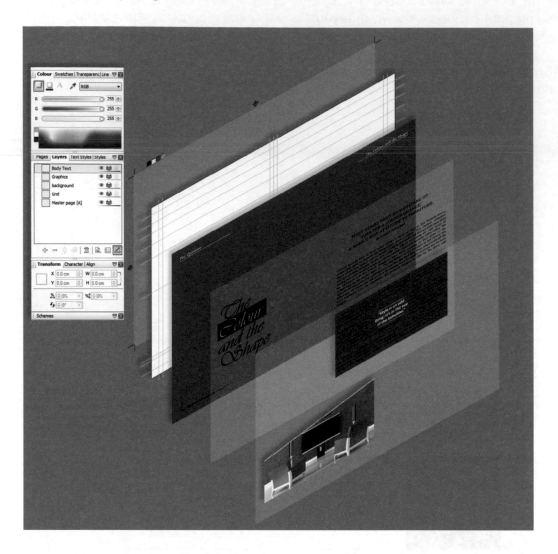

(c)   Describe layering as it is used in layout B in terms of the function and the benefits of layering for the graphic designer.

2

MARKS | DO NOT WRITE IN THIS MARGIN

7. **(continued)**

Examine **both** layout A and layout B.

Three DTP improvements have been made from layout A to layout B.

(d) Identify what these improvements are and explain their impact.

(i) | Layout improvement 1 is:

and the impact is:

2

(ii) | Layout improvement 2 is:

and the impact is:

2

(iii) | Layout improvement 3 is:

and the impact is:

2

[END OF SPECIMEN QUESTION PAPER]

Question 6 supplement

Layout 1

Layout 2

Layout 3

Question 7 supplement

Layout A

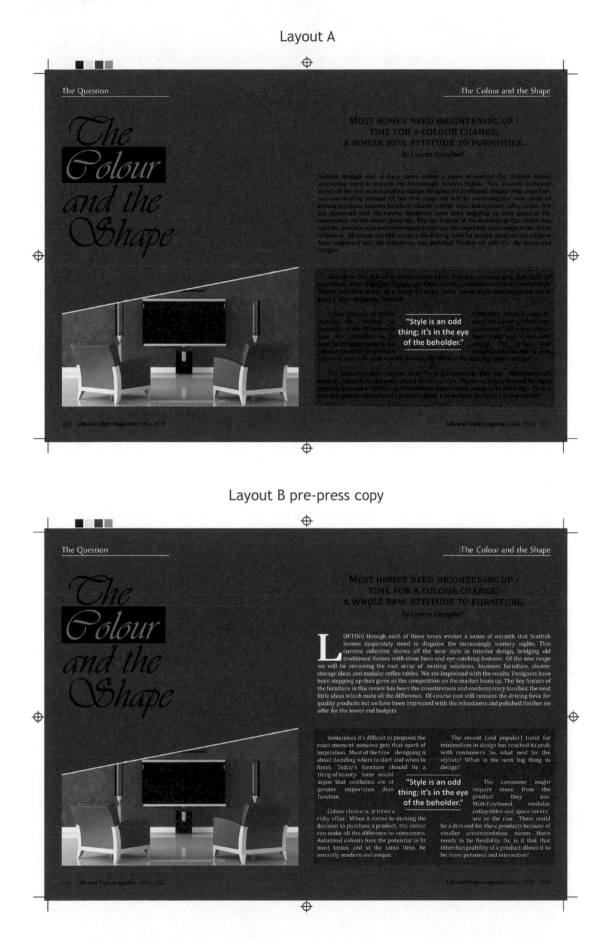

Layout B pre-press copy

ADDITIONAL SPACE FOR ANSWERS

MARKS | DO NOT WRITE IN THIS MARGIN

ADDITIONAL SPACE FOR ANSWERS

HIGHER FOR CfE

Model Paper 1

Whilst this Model Paper has been specially commissioned by Hodder Gibson for use as practice for the Higher (for Curriculum for Excellence) exams, the key reference documents remain the SQA Specimen Paper 2014 and SQA Past Paper 2015.

H

National Qualifications
MODEL PAPER 1

Mark

Graphic Communication

Duration — 2 hours

Fill in these boxes and read what is printed below.

Full name of centre

Town

Forename(s)

Surname

Number of seat

Date of birth

Day	Month	Year
D D	M M	Y Y

Scottish candidate number

Total marks — 70

Attempt ALL questions.

Write your answers clearly in the spaces provided in this booklet. Additional space for answers is provided at the end of this booklet. If you use this space you must clearly identify the question number you are attempting.

All dimensions are in mm.

All technical sketches and drawings use third angle projection.

You may use rulers, compasses or trammels for measuring.

In all questions you may use sketches and annotations to support your answer if you wish.

Use **blue** or **black** ink.

Before leaving the examination room you must give this booklet to the Invigilator; if you do not, you may lose all the marks for this paper.

Attempt ALL questions

Total marks — 70

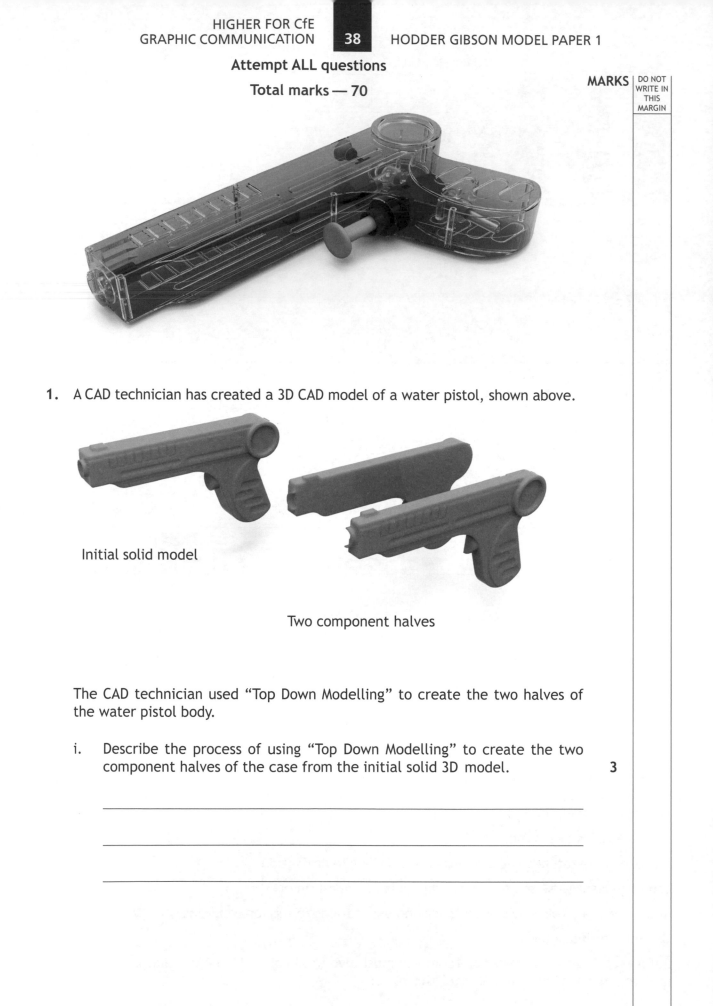

Initial solid model

Two component halves

1. A CAD technician has created a 3D CAD model of a water pistol, shown above.

The CAD technician used "Top Down Modelling" to create the two halves of the water pistol body.

i. Describe the process of using "Top Down Modelling" to create the two component halves of the case from the initial solid 3D model.

3

_____

_____

_____

MARKS | DO NOT WRITE IN THIS MARGIN

1. (continued)

Component design for plastic stopper
to seal the water reservoir.

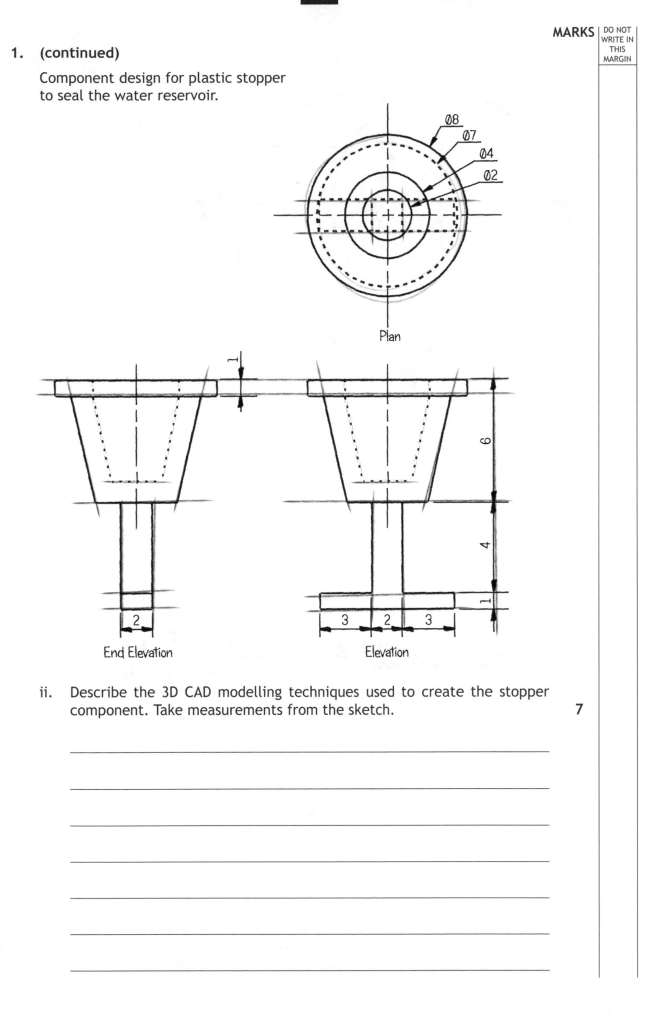

Plan

End Elevation

Elevation

ii. Describe the 3D CAD modelling techniques used to create the stopper
component. Take measurements from the sketch.

7

_____

_____

_____

_____

_____

_____

_____

1. (continued)

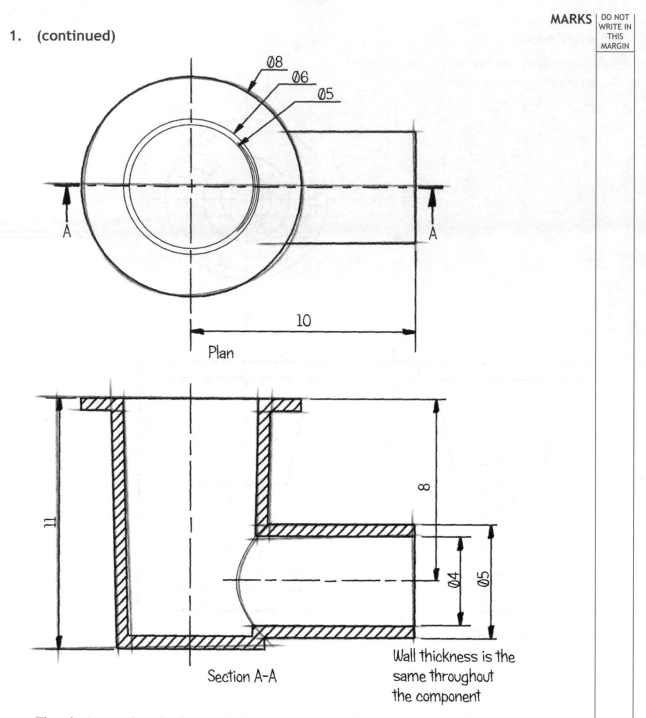

Plan

Section A-A

Wall thickness is the same throughout the component

The designer sketched one of the components for holding a pipe inside the water pistol.

iii. Describe the 3D CAD modelling techniques used to create the component. Take measurements from the sketch.

7

MARKS | DO NOT WRITE IN THIS MARGIN

1. (continued)

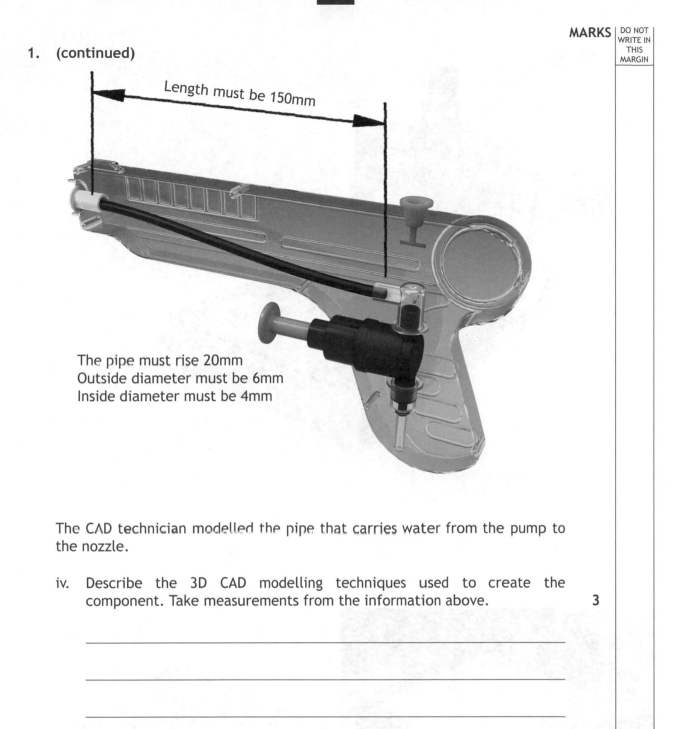

Length must be 150mm

The pipe must rise 20mm
Outside diameter must be 6mm
Inside diameter must be 4mm

The CAD technician modelled the pipe that carries water from the pump to the nozzle.

iv. Describe the 3D CAD modelling techniques used to create the component. Take measurements from the information above.

3

_____

_____

_____

1. (continued)

The CAD technician was asked to create a physical model from the 3D CAD model.

v.   State the term used when computer designs are used with machines to manufacture items.

1

The CAD technician created the foam prototype from the CAD model, above.

vi. Explain **one** advantage and **one** disadvantage of physical models compared to 3D CAD models.

2

MARKS | DO NOT WRITE IN THIS MARGIN

2.

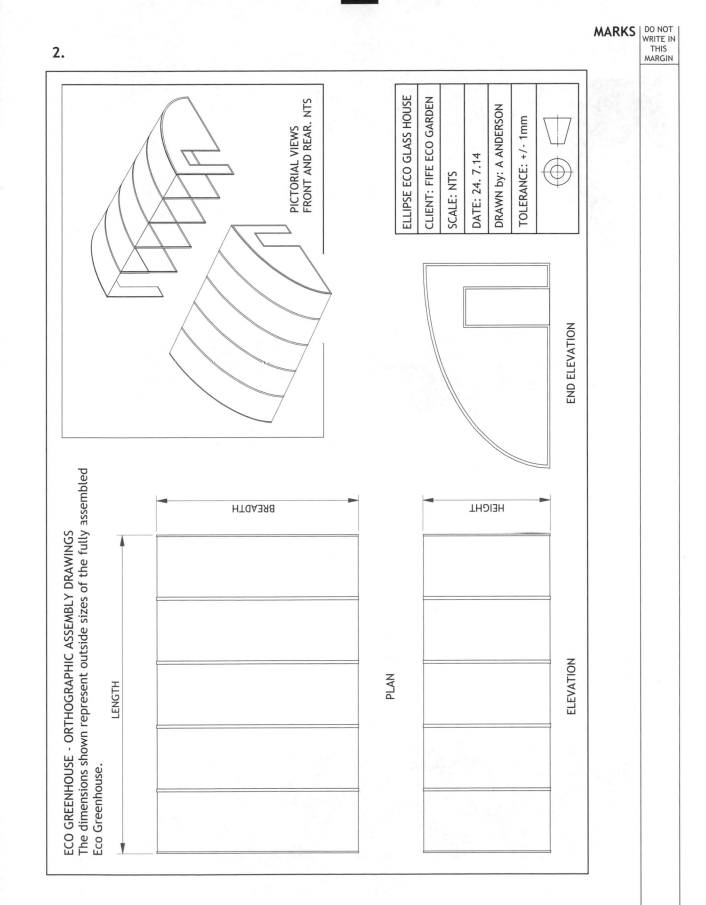

PICTORIAL VIEWS
FRONT AND REAR. NTS

| ELLIPSE ECO GLASS HOUSE |
| CLIENT: FIFE ECO GARDEN |
| SCALE: NTS |
| DATE: 24. 7.14 |
| DRAWN by: A ANDERSON |
| TOLERANCE: +/- 1mm |

END ELEVATION

ECO GREENHOUSE - ORTHOGRAPHIC ASSEMBLY DRAWINGS
The dimensions shown represent outside sizes of the fully assembled Eco Greenhouse.

LENGTH

BREADTH

HEIGHT

PLAN

ELEVATION

2. (continued)

Component details

The Eco Greenhouse has four main components. These are shown below.
The only dimensions shown are the main sizes of the perspex components.
The metal frames are built to fit around the perspex components snugly.
The greenhouse is modular and can have as many sections as are required.
Dimensions of the metal frames are shown on page nine.

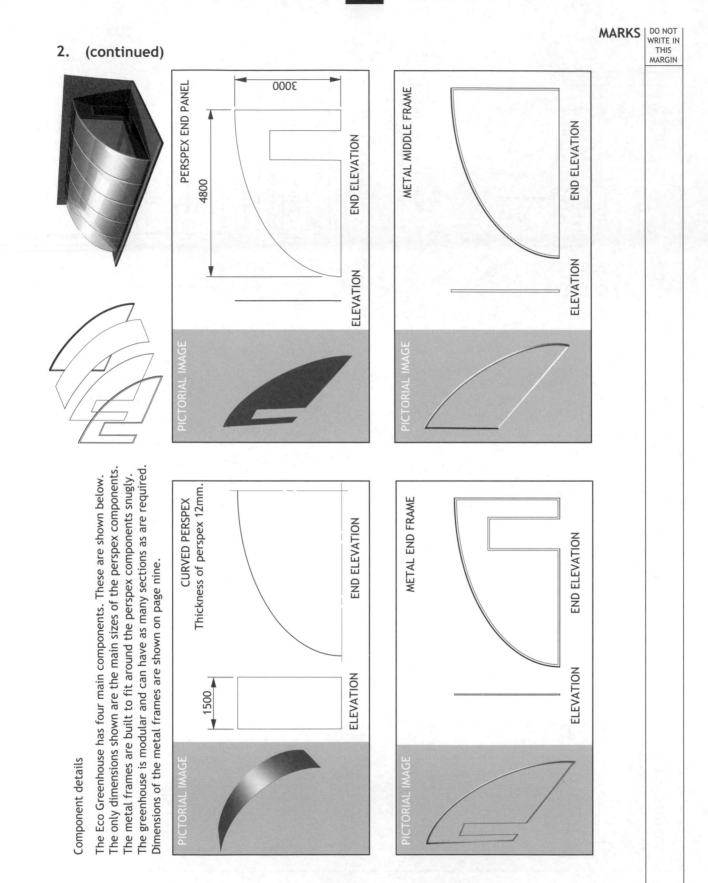

PERSPEX END PANEL

3000

4800

END ELEVATION

ELEVATION

PICTORIAL IMAGE

METAL MIDDLE FRAME

END ELEVATION

ELEVATION

PICTORIAL IMAGE

CURVED PERSPEX
Thickness of perspex 12mm.

END ELEVATION

1500

ELEVATION

PICTORIAL IMAGE

METAL END FRAME

END ELEVATION

ELEVATION

PICTORIAL IMAGE

2. (continued)

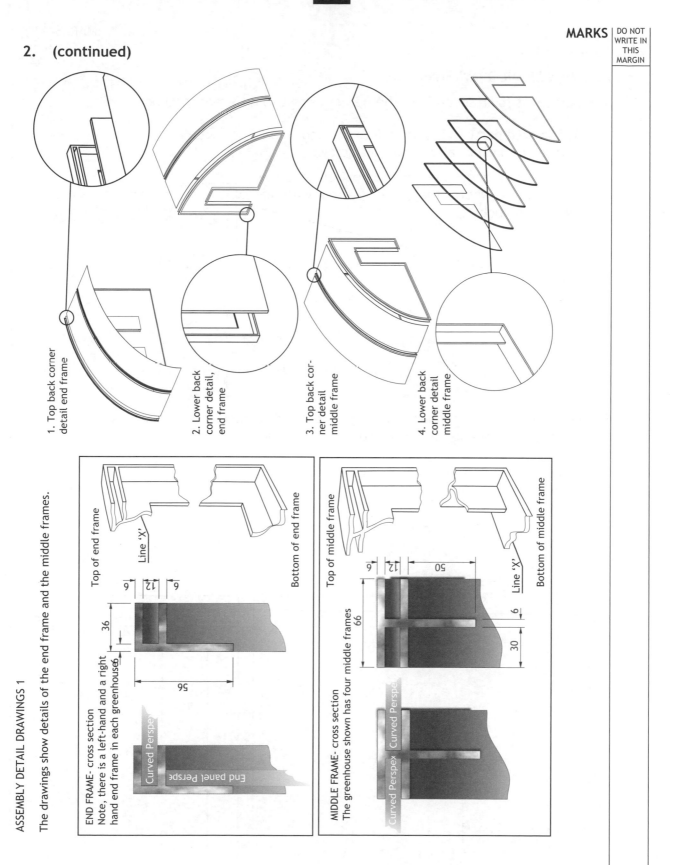

ASSEMBLY DETAIL DRAWINGS 1

The drawings show details of the end frame and the middle frames.

1. Top back corner detail end frame

2. Lower back corner detail, end frame

3. Top back corner detail middle frame

4. Lower back corner detail middle frame

Top of end frame

Line 'X'

Bottom of end frame

Top of middle frame

Bottom of middle frame

Line 'X'

END FRAME- cross section
Note, there is a left-hand and a right hand end frame in each greenhouse.

MIDDLE FRAME- cross section
The greenhouse shown has four middle frames

6
12
6
36
56

6
12
50
66
6
30

End panel Perspex
Curved Perspex

Curved Perspex
Curved Perspex

MARKS | DO NOT WRITE IN THIS MARGIN

2.   (continued)

ASSEMBLY DETAIL DRAWINGS 2

The perspex is fixed securely to the frames using two different methods.

- The curved perspex is slotted into the end frame and secured using an M8 machine screw.

- The perspex end panels are a neat fit into the end frames where they are secured with an M8 nut and bolt.

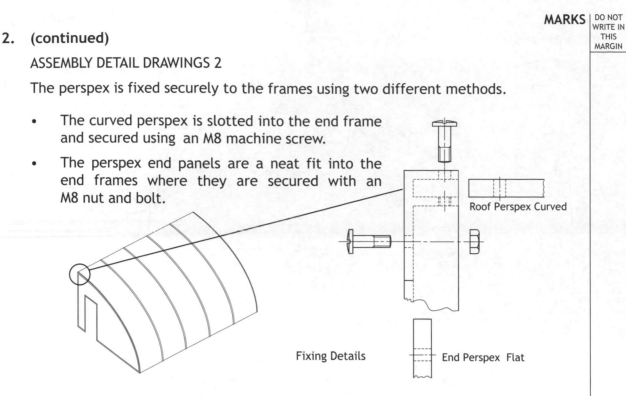

Roof Perspex Curved

Fixing Details   End Perspex Flat

Detailed assembly drawings showing assembled components have been drawn to support on-site assembly. Section A-A , below, is incomplete.

i.   Complete section A-A by cross-hatching it according to BS Drawing Standards and Conventions.

6

A

Line 'X'

A

SECTION A-A

MARKS | DO NOT WRITE IN THIS MARGIN

2. (continued)

Study the four pages of Component Drawings and the Assembly Detail Drawings carefully.

The overall dimensions after the greenhouse is assembled are important to provide planning information.

ii.   Calculate the overall assembled **length** of the 5 panel Eco Greenhouse. Give your answer in millimetres.   **1**

   Overall assembled length _____ mm

In the Assembly Detail Drawings, a line type called **line "X"** is used. It is described in Drawing Standards and Conventions as a *'Continuous, thin, irregular line'*.

iii.   Explain the function of this type of line in the assembly detail drawings.   **1**

_____

The Eco Greenhouse is a large structure and it was important to show assembly details.

iv.   State two of the graphical methods (types of drawings) that the designer has used to clarify the assembly details.

   Justify the graphical methods used by describing the benefits they provide.

   1 Graphical Method used to clarify the assembly details: _____   **1**

   Benefits of using this method _____   **1**

_____

_____

   2 Graphical Method used to clarify the assembly details: _____   **1**

   Benefits of using this method _____   **1**

_____

_____

MARKS | DO NOT WRITE IN THIS MARGIN

2. **(continued)**

The Eco Greenhouse is being installed against a wall of the bungalow shown below. The plan view and elevation of the bungalow are given.

v.   Identify the missing **end elevations** from the eight views shown below.   **2**

(You may sketch solutions to help you work out your answers).

LEFT END ELEVATION is view _____

RIGHT END ELEVATION is view _____

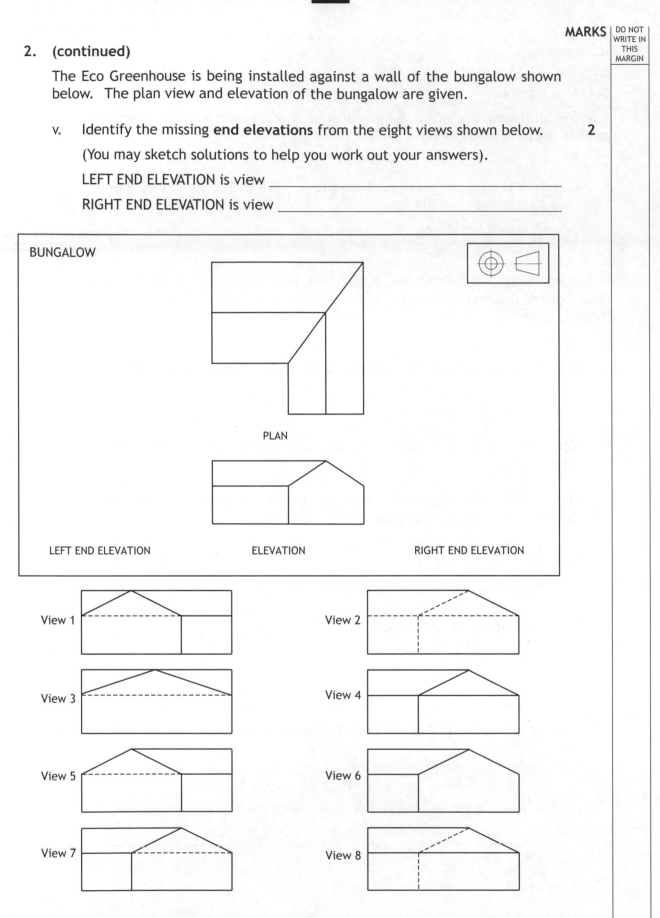

MARKS | DO NOT WRITE IN THIS MARGIN

2. **(continued)**

Additional (auxiliary) elevations are required for the planning application.

vi. Identify the two missing auxiliary elevations from the eight views shown below.   **2**

(You may sketch solutions to help you work out your answers).

AUXILIARY ELEVATION 1 is view _____

AUXILIARY ELEVATION 2 is view _____

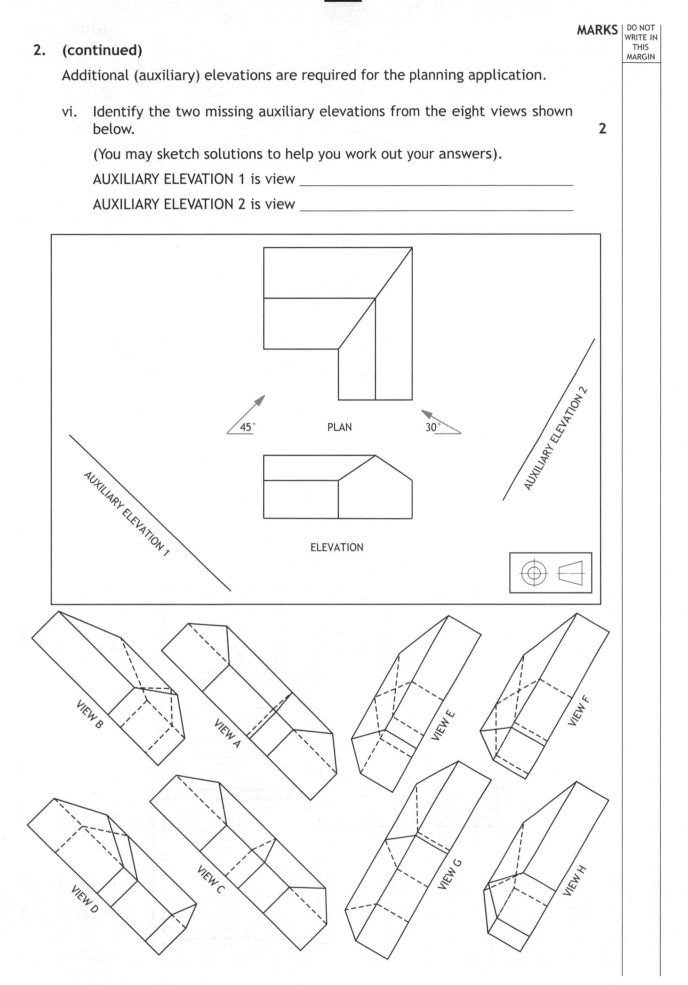

MARKS | DO NOT WRITE IN THIS MARGIN

2.   (continued)

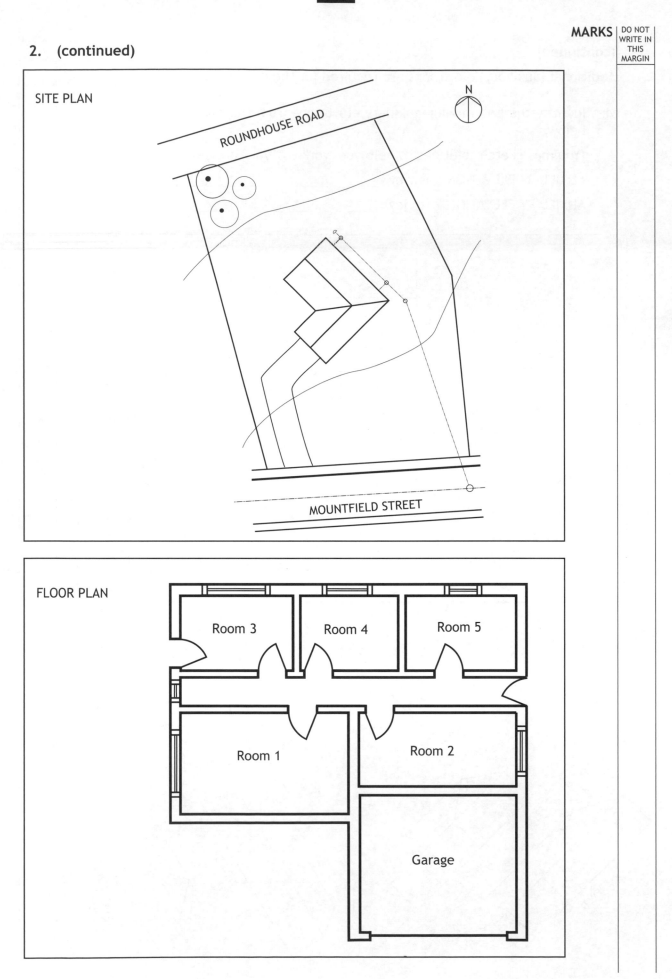

SITE PLAN

N

ROUNDHOUSE ROAD

MOUNTFIELD STREET

FLOOR PLAN

Room 3

Room 4

Room 5

Room 1

Room 2

Garage

MARKS | DO NOT WRITE IN THIS MARGIN

2.   (continued)

The bungalow is a two bedroom house. The site plan and a part completed floor plan are shown on the previous page. Study them both before answering the questions below.

The Eco Greenhouse is to be assembled against a wall of the bungalow. For best results the wall should face in a south-west direction.

vii. Identify the wall that best meets the requirements of the Eco Greenhouse.

Sketch or annotate the position of the Eco Greenhouse on the site plan.   **1**

The content of rooms is in the process of being finalised but the function of each room has been decided.

viii. Identify the position of the kitchen and bathroom in the bungalow.

The kitchen is planned for room number _____   **1**

The bathroom is planned for room number _____   **1**

ix.   Explain how you identified these rooms as the kitchen and bathroom.

I identified the kitchen because: _____   **1**

_____

I identified the bathroom because: _____   **1**

_____

MARKS | DO NOT WRITE IN THIS MARGIN

3. Adventure Plus sell outdoor camping and walking equipment. A freelance graphic designer has been asked to create a promotional advert to be published in "THE GREAT OUTDOORS" magazine. The company decides what text and images will be used and the graphic designer creates a layout using this material. The designer's approach is to put together a draft layout. He then applies his knowledge of design elements and principles and DTP features to create a layout that has visual impact.

The draft layout and the final published layout are shown below.

First Draft layout
The draft layout shows the components of the layout in their original size and form.

Published layout
The published layout is the final layout that is published in the magazine.

MARKS | DO NOT WRITE IN THIS MARGIN

3. (continued)

Design elements and principles are often applied in a layout by using DTP techniques. The following questions ask you to identify the DTP features that are used when the designer applies design elements and principles to the published layout.

The graphic designer had to establish unity in the layout and used DTP techniques to achieve this.

i. Describe two DTP techniques the designer used to create **unity** in the **published layout**.

2

Emphasis is important in any promotional layout.

ii. Describe two ways in which the designer has created **emphasis** in the **published layout**.

2

The use of contrast can make or break a layout; the use of red and green colours achieves contrast.

iii. Describe two methods, other than using colour, which the designer has used to create **contrast** in the layout

2

Despite incorporating different shapes and positioning, the layout looks well organised and flows well from the top to the bottom.

iv. Explain how the designer achieved an **organised** and **structured** look to the layout.

1

MARKS | DO NOT WRITE IN THIS MARGIN

3. **(continued)**

The text in the published layout has been arranged in a hierarchy (level of importance).

v.   Discuss how this hierarchy (level of importance) is achieved and how it makes the layout easier to navigate through.   **2**

_____

_____

_____

The typefaces used in the layout have been chosen for a particular purpose.

vi.   Describe how the choice of typeface supports the function of each section of text   **3**

Title: _____

_____

Sub-Head: _____

_____

Body text: _____

_____

The published layout makes use of a "partial-bleed".

vii. Explain the term "partial-bleed".   **2**

_____

_____

_____

The promotional layout is designed to help sell "Adventure Plus" products but it also encourages people to adopt a healthy lifestyle.

viii. Describe how the layout puts this message across to potential customers.   **1**

_____

_____

ix.   State one method the company have employed to make the activity inclusive.   **1**

_____

_____

MARKS | DO NOT WRITE IN THIS MARGIN

4. A national UK charity called **"Make a home for Bees"**, has commissioned a poster for a campaign to raise awareness of the decline of bumblebees and honey bees. The campaign encourages ordinary people to create habitat for our declining bee population. The poster will be displayed on roadside and high street bill-boards.

Study the poster and answer the following questions.

MARKS | DO NOT WRITE IN THIS MARGIN

4. (continued)

The designer has established a connection between the health of the bee population and maintaining our own way of life.

i.   Explain how the designer achieved this connection in the poster.   **2**

_____

_____

Contrast is often used to make a layout more eye-catching .

Contrast can also be used to deliver a message, in this case an ecological and environmental message.

ii. Explain how contrast in graphics and images have been used to put a strong environmental message across.   **1**

_____

_____

The designer felt it was important to make the poster as 3-dimensional as possible and made an effort to create depth in the poster.

iii. Describe three DTP techniques that have been used to achieve depth in the layout.   **3**

_____

_____

_____

In promotional posters a balance is struck between the amount of text and the extent of the images used.

iv. Explain why the textual information in this poster has been kept to a minimum   **2**

_____

_____

The designer has made full use of his DTP skills by editing the text used in the slogans.

v.   Describe and justify a DTP editing technique used on the slogans in the layout.   **2**

Description of text editing technique _____

_____

Justification _____

[END OF MODEL PAPER]

Model Paper 2

Whilst this Model Paper has been specially commissioned by Hodder Gibson for use as practice for the Higher (for Curriculum for Excellence) exams, the key reference documents remain the SQA Specimen Paper 2014 and SQA Past Paper 2015.

National Qualifications
MODEL PAPER 2

Mark

Graphic Communication

Duration — 2 hours

Fill in these boxes and read what is printed below.

Full name of centre

Town

Forename(s)

Surname

Number of seat

Date of birth
Day   Month   Year

D D M M Y Y

Scottish candidate number

Total marks — 70

Attempt ALL questions.

Write your answers clearly in the spaces provided in this booklet. Additional space for answers is provided at the end of this booklet. If you use this space you must clearly identify the question number you are attempting.

All dimensions are in mm.

All technical sketches and drawings use third angle projection.

You may use rulers, compasses or trammels for measuring.

In all questions you may use sketches and annotations to support your answer if you wish.

Use **blue** or **black** ink.

Before leaving the examination room you must give this booklet to the Invigilator; if you do not, you may lose all the marks for this paper.

HODDER
GIBSON
LEARN MORE

Attempt ALL questions

Total marks — 70

MARKS | DO NOT WRITE IN THIS MARGIN

1. A CAD technician has created a 3D CAD model of a candle holder.

   All the components and features were sketched before making a 3D CAD model.

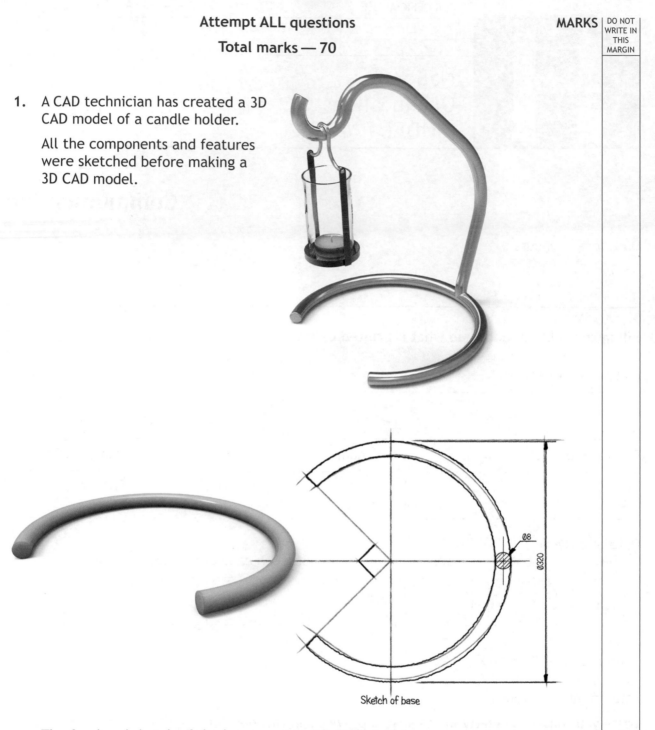

Sketch of base

The freehand sketch of the base component is shown above.

   i.   Describe the 3D CAD modelling techniques used to create the base.
         Take measurements from the sketch.   **3**

   _____

   _____

   _____

MARKS | DO NOT WRITE IN THIS MARGIN

1.   (continued)

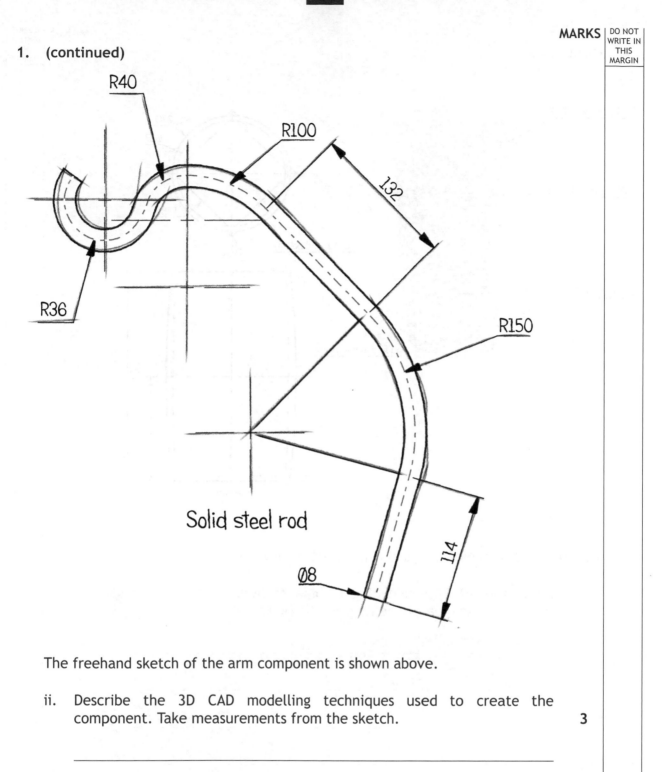

Solid steel rod

The freehand sketch of the arm component is shown above.

ii.   Describe the 3D CAD modelling techniques used to create the
     component. Take measurements from the sketch.   **3**

_____

_____

_____

MARKS | DO NOT WRITE IN THIS MARGIN

1. (continued)

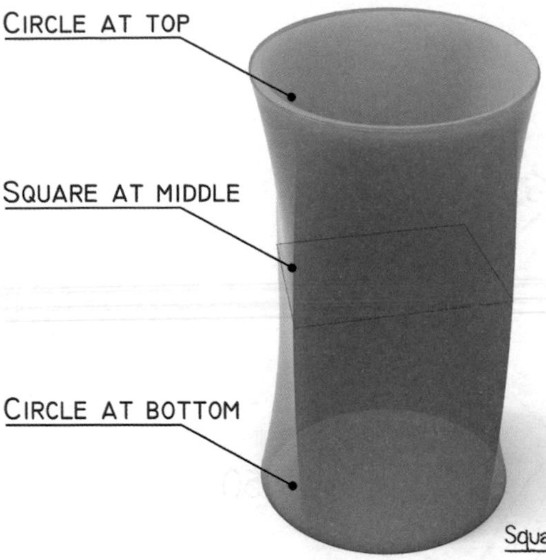

CIRCLE AT TOP

SQUARE AT MIDDLE

CIRCLE AT BOTTOM

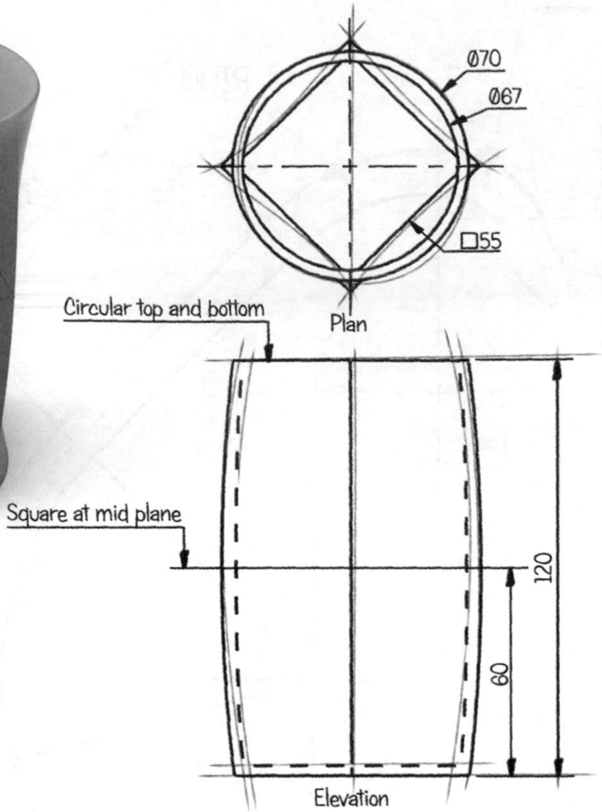

Ø70
Ø67
□55

Circular top and bottom   Plan

Square at mid plane

120
60

Elevation

The freehand sketch of the glass component is shown above.

iii. Describe the 3D CAD modelling techniques used to create the glass component. Take measurements from the sketch.

7

_____

_____

_____

_____

_____

_____

_____

_____

1. (continued)

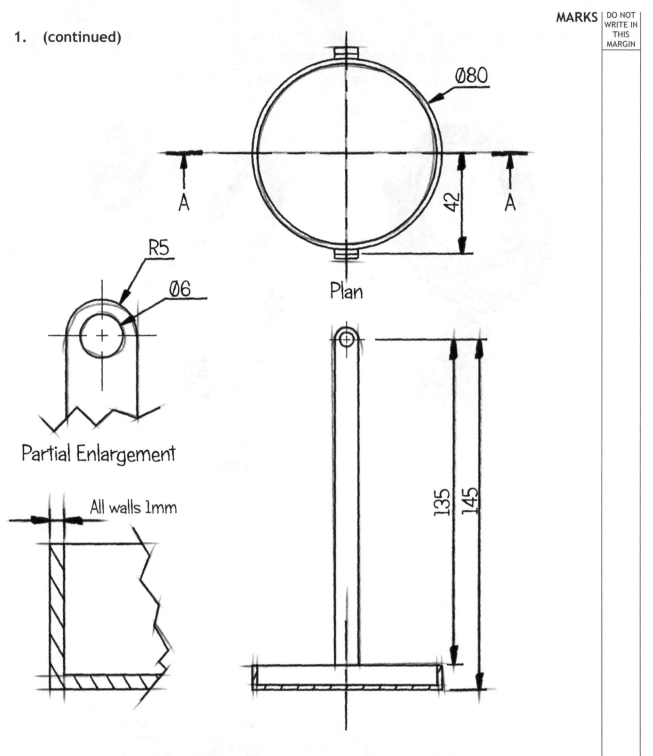

Plan

R5

Ø6

Ø80

42

Partial Enlargement

All walls 1mm

135

145

The freehand sketch of the cradle component is shown on the previous page. The cradle is a single component.

iv. Describe the 3D CAD modelling techniques used to create the cradle component. Take measurements from the sketch.

7

MARKS | DO NOT WRITE IN THIS MARGIN

2. Illustrations and drawings of the "OUI Mirror", a new swivel desk mirror are shown. A parts list describes the individual components.

Study the information on this page carefully and answer the following questions.

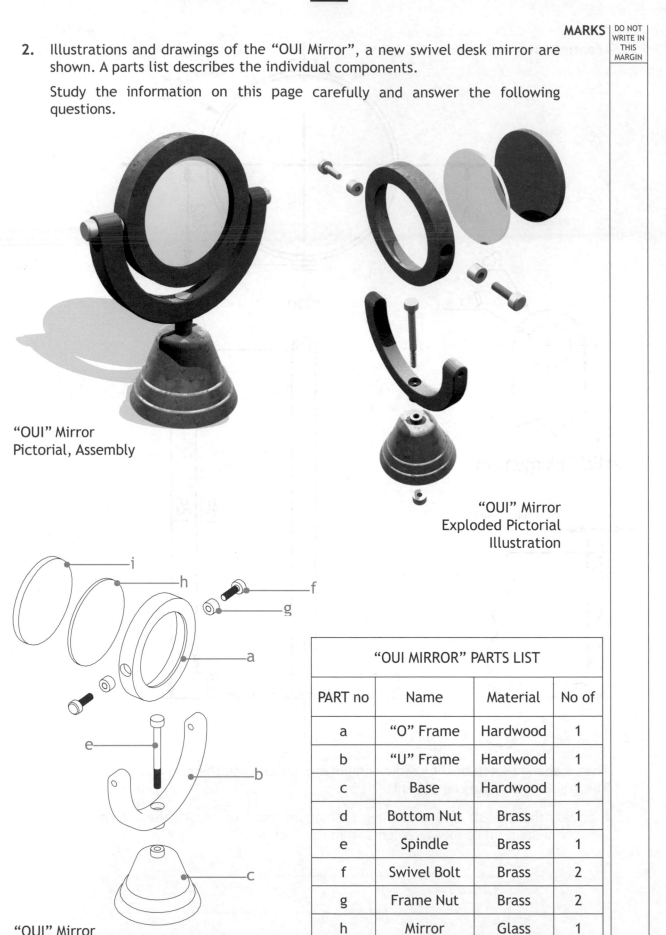

"OUI" Mirror
Pictorial, Assembly

"OUI" Mirror
Exploded Pictorial
Illustration

"OUI" Mirror
Pictorial, Exploded
Line Drawing

"OUI MIRROR" PARTS LIST			
PART no	Name	Material	No of
a	"O" Frame	Hardwood	1
b	"U" Frame	Hardwood	1
c	Base	Hardwood	1
d	Bottom Nut	Brass	1
e	Spindle	Brass	1
f	Swivel Bolt	Brass	2
g	Frame Nut	Brass	2
h	Mirror	Glass	1
i	Backboard	Plywood	1

2. (continued)

Sectional views have been created to give the manufacturer more information about the assembly of the mirror. Study the sectional views carefully.

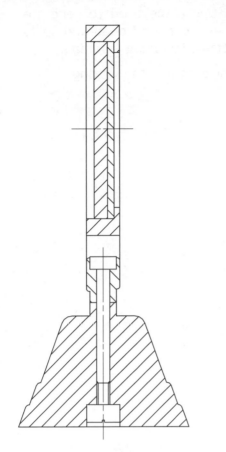

SECTION A-A

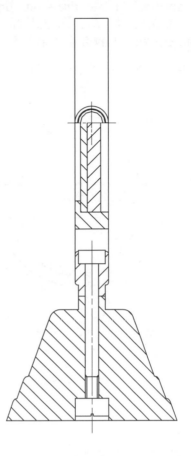

SECTION B-B

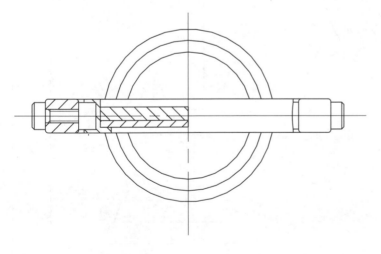

SECTION C-C

2. (continued)

Orthographic assembly drawings are shown below.

i. Describe, on the drawings below, the cutting plane used to generate **SECTION A-A**. You should show exactly where it is positioned and apply the correct drawing standards and conventions, including labelling.

You may sketch or draw the cutting plane or describe it in writing.

2

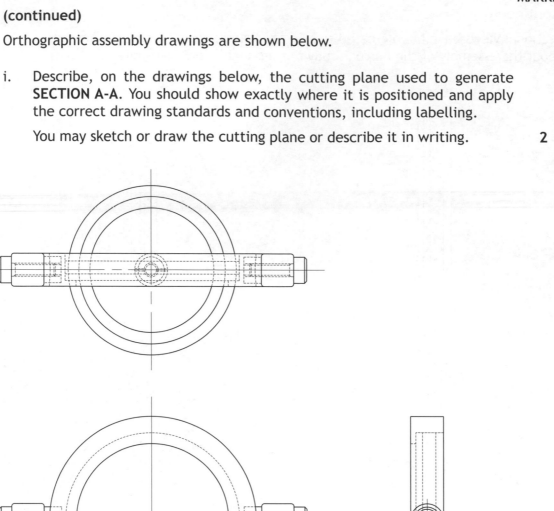

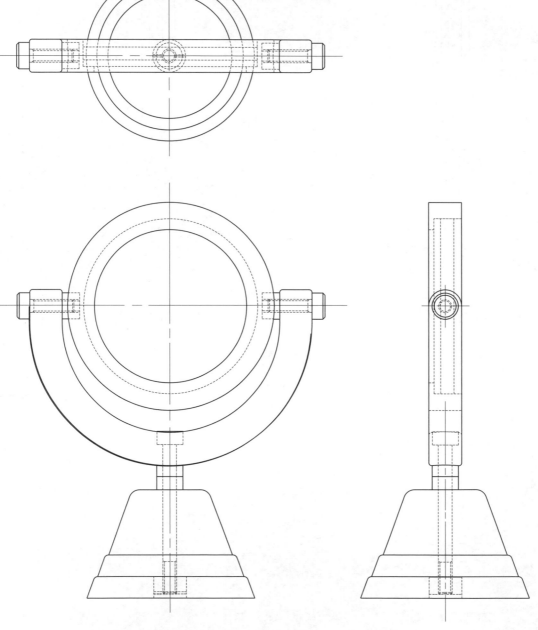

2. (continued)

Orthographic assembly drawings are shown below.

ii. Describe, on the drawings below, the cutting plane used to generate **SECTION B-B**. You should show exactly where it is positioned and apply the correct drawing standards and conventions, including labelling.

You may sketch or draw the cutting plane or describe it in writing.

2

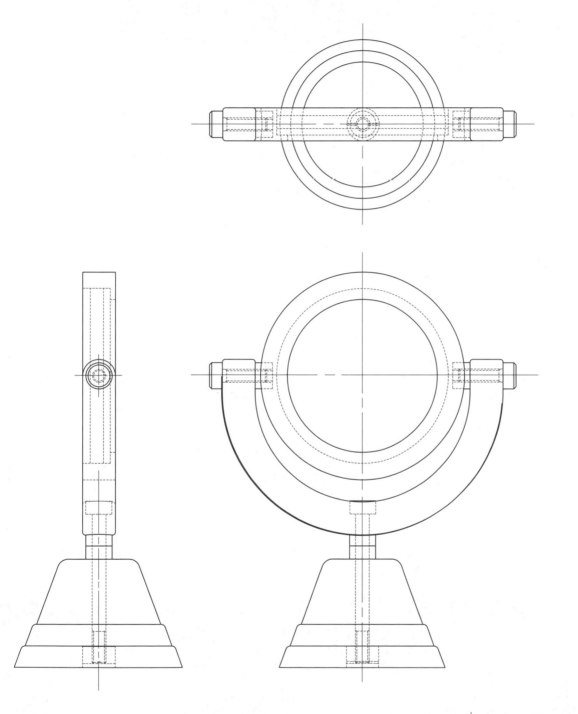

2. **(continued)**

Orthographic assembly drawings are shown below.

iii. Describe, on the drawings below, the cutting plane used to generate **SECTION C-C**. You should show exactly where it is positioned and apply the correct drawing standards and conventions, including labelling.

You may sketch or draw the cutting plane or describe it in writing.

2

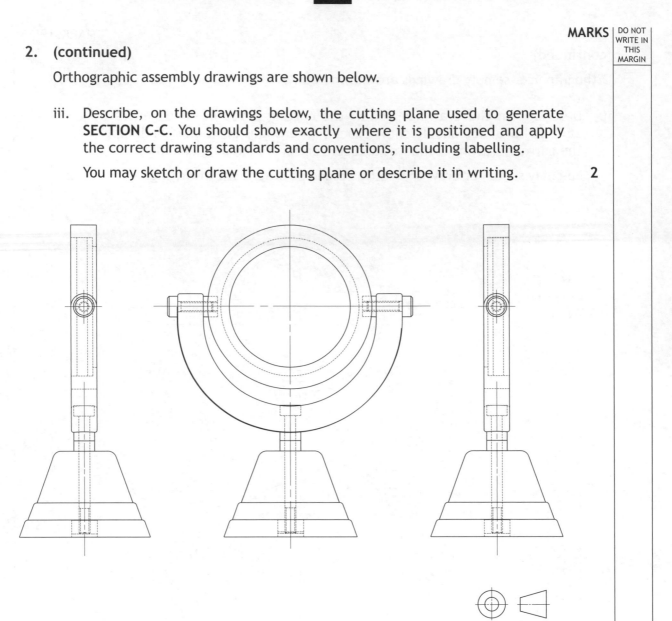

MARKS | DO NOT WRITE IN THIS MARGIN

2. (continued)

Scaled drawings of components from the "OUI" Mirror are shown below.

The spindle has to be the correct length so that it secures the bottom nut and holds the assembly together. The functional length of the spindle is the length from the underside of the head.

iv. Calculate the **maximum** functional length of the spindle to allow it to work properly. You can measure the scaled components below to help you arrive at your answer.

1

v. Add the dimension to the drawing of the spindle. Apply appropriate drawing standards and conventions.

1

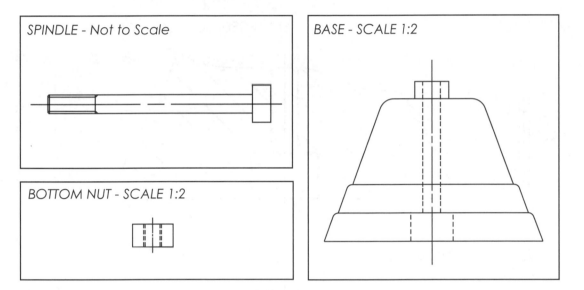

SPINDLE - Not to Scale

BASE - SCALE 1:2

BOTTOM NUT - SCALE 1:2

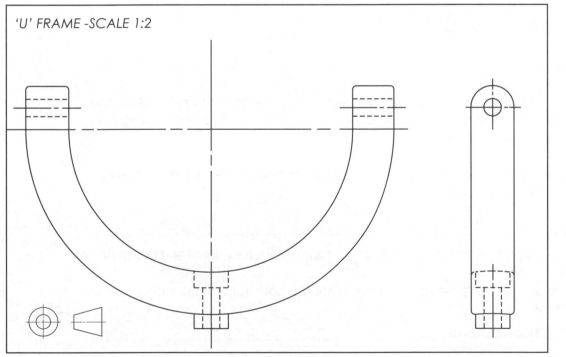

'U' FRAME -SCALE 1:2

MARKS | DO NOT WRITE IN THIS MARGIN

2. (continued)

During manufacture the mirror is produced in batches and packaged in a flat-pack format.

The bottom hole in the base is Ø30 in size. The bottom nut is also Ø30 in size. If they are both the same size the parts will not fit together. A suitable tolerance needs to be applied to the dimensions of both parts.

vi. Describe suitable tolerances that would be applied to the outside diameter of the bottom nut and the bottom hole. You can dimension the nut and the bottom hole on the enlarged sectional view and add the tolerances to your dimensions.

Apply the correct drawing standards and conventions to your answer. 3

EXPLODED, SECTIONAL VIEW   ENLARGED, SECTIONAL VIEW

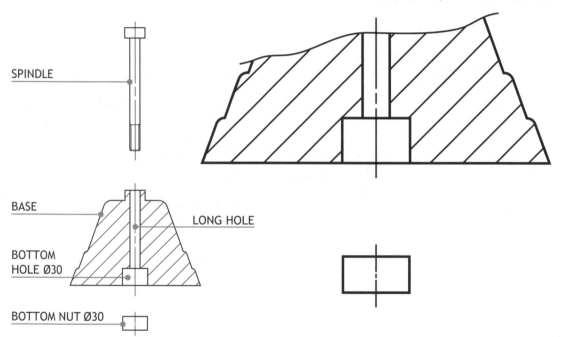

SPINDLE

BASE

LONG HOLE

BOTTOM HOLE Ø30

BOTTOM NUT Ø30

The bottom hole in the base of the mirror has a bigger diameter than the long hole for the spindle. This feature is given a recognised name, described in drawing standards and conventions.

vii. State the recognised name of the bottom hole as described in drawing standards and conventions. 1

_____

The purpose of the bottom hole in the base is both **functional** and **cosmetic**.

viii. Explain the purpose of the bottom hole in both functional and cosmetic terms. 2

Functional purpose: _____

_____

Cosmetic purpose: _____

_____

2. (continued)

A sectional, exploded view of part of the mirror is shown.

The 45° hatching lines in both areas of cross-hatching shown on the sectional detail, travel in the same direction.

ix. State what piece of information this gives about the cross-hatched areas, other than, they have both been cut.

1

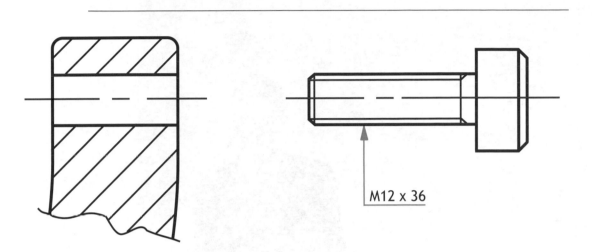

M12 x 36

A drawing standards symbol (i) was added to the head of the swivel bolt.

x. Explain the meaning of this symbol

1

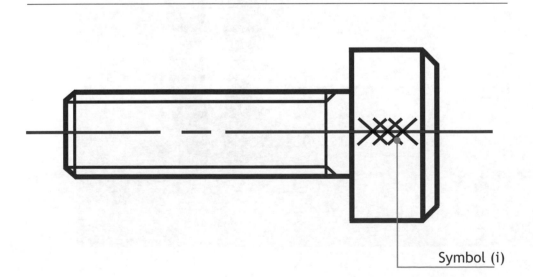

Symbol (i)

3.

Layout 1

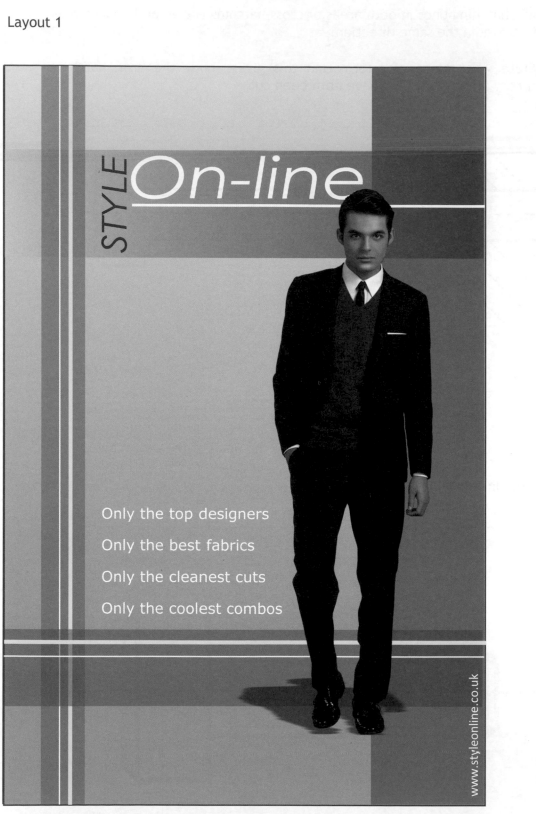

3. **(continued)**

Layout 2

MARKS | DO NOT WRITE IN THIS MARGIN

3.   (continued)

"Style On-line" is a clothing retailer aiming to sell to a young stylish target market. They offer a range of clothing for men and women. A full page flyer (leaflet) with a 5000 print run is to be produced and distributed in high streets.

Two versions of the flyer have been submitted to the marketing team for approval.

The graphic designer considered design elements and principles when she created the layouts.   Balance is used differently in each of the layouts.

i.   Compare the use of balance in each of the layouts giving advantages and disadvantages of each method.   4

The layouts are monochrome, using only greys and white. The designer had to come up with other ways of creating contrast.

ii.   Describe two other ways in which the designer has created contrast in layout 1.   2

The designer has made use of several DTP techniques in the layouts.

The background fills have been edited to create a subtle, textured effect.

iii.   Describe the DTP editing techniques used to create the grey background fills.   2

The outfit that the model is wearing is dark grey in colour. The colour chosen for the monochrome backgrounds is also grey.

iv.   Explain why the designer chose grey for the backgrounds.   1

Both layouts were created over a DTP grid.

v.   Describe two possible benefits of using a grid to prepare a layout.   2

MARKS | DO NOT WRITE IN THIS MARGIN

3. (continued)

Preparing a document for a commercial print run requires setting up the file ready for printing. This is known as pre-press.

The pre-press print set-up for layout 1 reveals a number of details shown below.

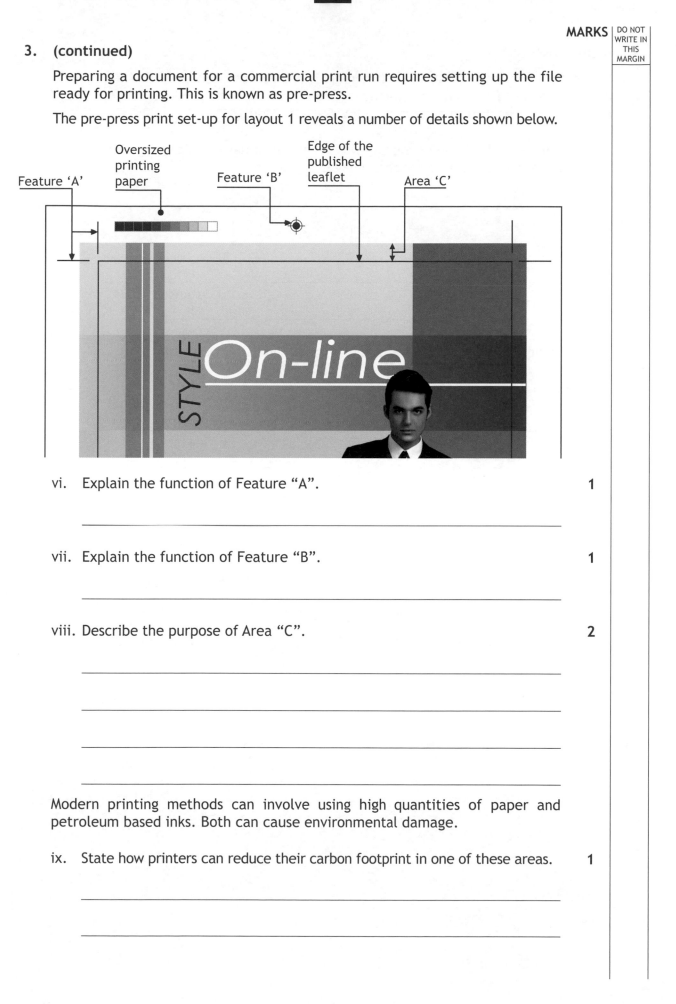

vi. Explain the function of Feature "A".   **1**

_____

vii. Explain the function of Feature "B".   **1**

_____

viii. Describe the purpose of Area "C".   **2**

_____

_____

_____

_____

Modern printing methods can involve using high quantities of paper and petroleum based inks. Both can cause environmental damage.

ix. State how printers can reduce their carbon footprint in one of these areas.   **1**

_____

_____

MARKS | DO NOT WRITE IN THIS MARGIN

3. (continued)

"Style On-Line" require several photographic images of each item in their clothing range. The company will have two copies of each product image, one at a **high-resolution** and one at a **lower-resolution.**

x. Explain why the online company would choose to have two photographs at different resolutions for each image.

2

_____

_____

_____

_____

The company has decided to "watermark" their high quality images.

xi. Explain why they might do this.

1

_____

_____

MARKS | DO NOT WRITE IN THIS MARGIN

4. MAKE is a popular magazine for people interesting in design and technology. The publisher sells the magazine globally and is continually looking to increase its readership.

MAKE publish the magazine in hard copy, along with having a pay-to-access website version.

i. Describe two advantages of hard-copy editions of magazines.   2

_____

_____

The magazine is desktop published in the USA, although features and articles are written by journalists in countries all around the world.

ii. Explain an advantage and disadvantage of this approach to creating a publication.   2

_____

_____

The publisher of MAKE sells advertising space on various pages of the magazine. The same advertisements also appear in the online edition. Selling advertisement space is an opportunity for the publisher to improve profits.

iii. Describe other advantages for the publisher of printing advertisements in the hard-copy edition of the magazine.   2

_____

_____

iv. Describe advantages to the advertiser of inserting advertisements in the online version of the magazine.   2

_____

_____

5. The layout below is a thumbnail design for a single page article on a rock band called DANZIG. The graphic designer has submitted this early layout to the magazine's editor for approval.

ROCK BAND MAGAZINE

THE WORLD AWAITS
DANZIG

Danzig's impending tour and album are due out this month to much hyped anticipation. The growing fan-base are already planning to attend pre-views of the album and the word-of -mouth gigs the band are planning in the run up to the launch in October. Lead singer Hector Rylance explained that the band have high hopes for the album and the excitement is building in the run-up to both the album's launch and the European tour in November. Several rival indie bands have already said they would love the support slot on Danzig's tour and have already been in touch with the bands management. However, the band themselves favour 'Heavy Water', their label stable-mates at Zeus records. Rylance himself said the band have a great rapport with them and their audience would approve having 'Heavy water' support on this tour. The tour itself takes in eight European countries including the UK, Germany, France, Spain and the Netherlands. It is already a sell out and the band expect a great reception in those countries they have toured before. Never before has a UK band had a number one with their debut album in so many countries around the globe. Danzig know they are in a strong position and that the pressure is on to repeat this success with the traditionally 'difficult second album'. However, they are ready

for it says singer Rylance, "We know the challenges and the pressure and we will respond positively." He went on to tell me, "We've already got 10 songs ready for the studio and are slotting some in to the set on the tour to bed them in." It bodes well for the future and the band

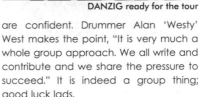

DANZIG ready for the tour

are confident. Drummer Alan 'Westy' West makes the point, "It is very much a whole group approach. We all write and contribute and we share the pressure to succeed." It is indeed a group thing; good luck lads.

34   www.rockbandmag.co.uk

MARKS | DO NOT WRITE IN THIS MARGIN

5.   (continued)

The magazine's editor feels that the designer needs to do more with text to draw the reader into the article. The layout needs something to bridge the gap, visually, between the title and the body text.

i.   Describe two options the designer might take to bridge the gap, visually, between the title and the body text   **2**

_____

_____

_____

The editor remarked that the image of the band needs to have more **emphasis** in the layout and suggested making it larger.

ii.   Describe **three other** DTP edits the designer may use to emphasise the photograph of the band.   **3**

_____

_____

_____

The editor observed that, while the font size and typeface are good, the body text lacks visual interest and looks daunting to the reader.

iii.   Describe two ways in which the designer could make the body text more visually appealing and less daunting to look at and read.   **2**

_____

_____

_____

[END OF MODEL PAPER]

Model Paper 3

Whilst this Model Paper has been specially commissioned by Hodder Gibson for use as practice for the Higher (for Curriculum for Excellence) exams, the key reference documents remain the SQA Specimen Paper 2014 and SQA Past Paper 2015.

HODDER
GIBSON
LEARN MORE

H

National
Qualifications
MODEL PAPER 3

Mark

Graphic
Communication

Duration — 2 hours

Fill in these boxes and read what is printed below.

Full name of centre

Town

Forename(s)

Surname

Number of seat

Date of birth
Day   Month   Year

D D   M M   Y Y

Scottish candidate number

Total marks — 70

Attempt ALL questions.

Write your answers clearly in the spaces provided in this booklet. Additional space for answers is provided at the end of this booklet. If you use this space you must clearly identify the question number you are attempting.

All dimensions are in mm.

All technical sketches and drawings use third angle projection.

You may use rulers, compasses or trammels for measuring.

In all questions you may use sketches and annotations to support your answer if you wish.

Use **blue** or **black** ink.

Before leaving the examination room you must give this booklet to the Invigilator; if you do not, you may lose all the marks for this paper.

Attempt ALL questions

Total marks — 70

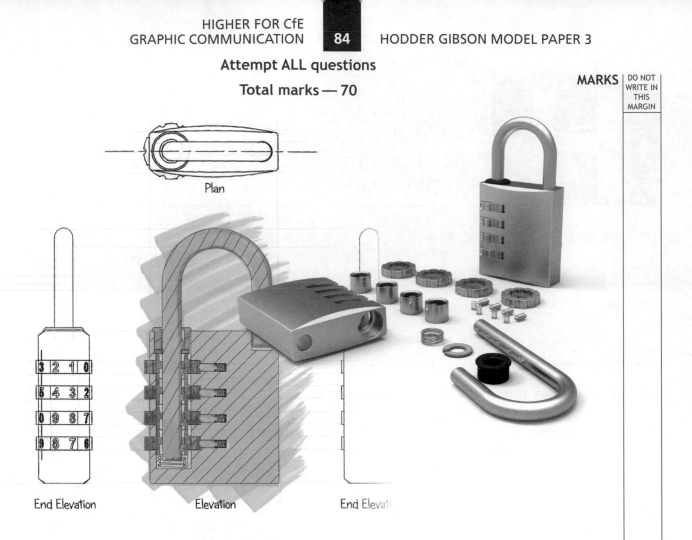

Plan

End Elevation   Elevation   End Elevati

1. A CAD technician was asked to create a 3D CAD model of a padlock from information provided on some freehand, preliminary sketches.

   The 3D CAD model was used used to make photo-realistic images of the padlock design.

   i.   Describe two functions that the 3D CAD could be used for, other than promotional illustrations.   **4**

   _____

   _____

   _____

   _____

1. (continued)

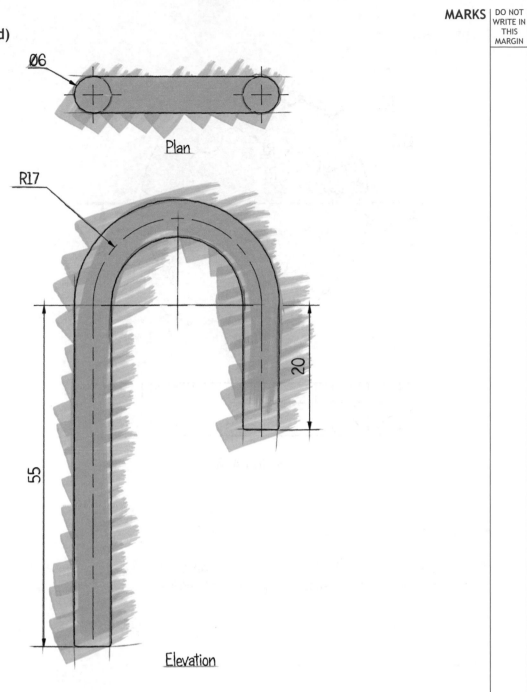

The freehand sketch of the latch component is shown above.

ii. Describe the 3D CAD modelling techniques used to create the latch component. Take measurements from the sketch.

3

_____

_____

_____

1. **(continued)**

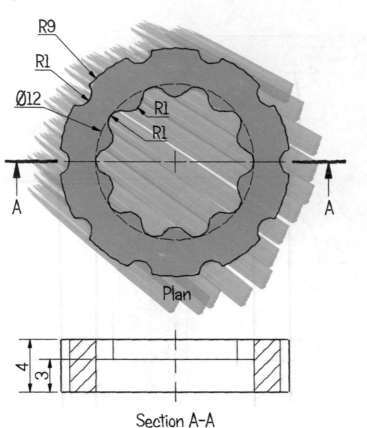

Plan

Section A-A

The freehand sketch of the dial component is shown above.

iii. Describe the 3D CAD modelling techniques used to create the dial
      component. Take measurements from the sketch.   **6**

_____

_____

_____

_____

_____

_____

1. **(continued)**

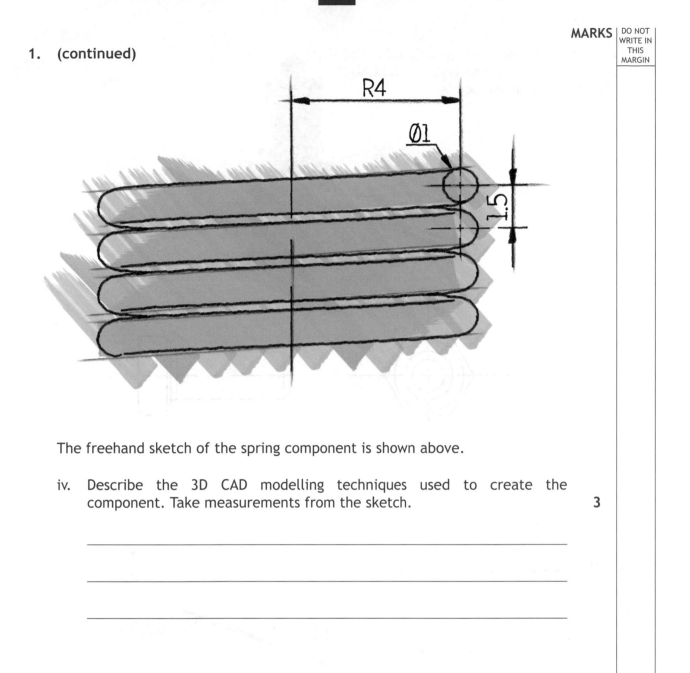

The freehand sketch of the spring component is shown above.

iv. Describe the 3D CAD modelling techniques used to create the component. Take measurements from the sketch.

3

_____

_____

_____

MARKS | DO NOT WRITE IN THIS MARGIN

2. A mechanical engineer has created a 3D CAD model of a small pump system. The CAD illustration is shown below.

END ELEVATION   ELEVATION

The pump uses bolts to assemble various components.

Apply the British Standard convention for a screw thread to both views of the bolt above.   2

26±0,5   126±0,25

PLAN

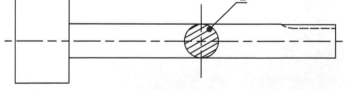

ELEVATION

The mechanical engineer created a 3D model of the component above. This size of this component is critical to the function of the pump.

i.   Calculate the maximum full length of the component..   1

_____

ii. Calculate the minimum full length of the component..   1

_____

MARKS | DO NOT WRITE IN THIS MARGIN

2. **(continued)**

iii. Explain the purpose of the technical detail shown at "A" on the previous page.

3

_____

_____

_____

An exploded view of the pump system is shown above.

The mechanical engineer created an elevation and sectional assembly drawing of the pump. These are shown on the next page.

iv. Apply the appropriate cross hatch marks to the sectional view. Do not section the bolts.

6

v. Apply three missing centre lines.

3

2.   (continued)

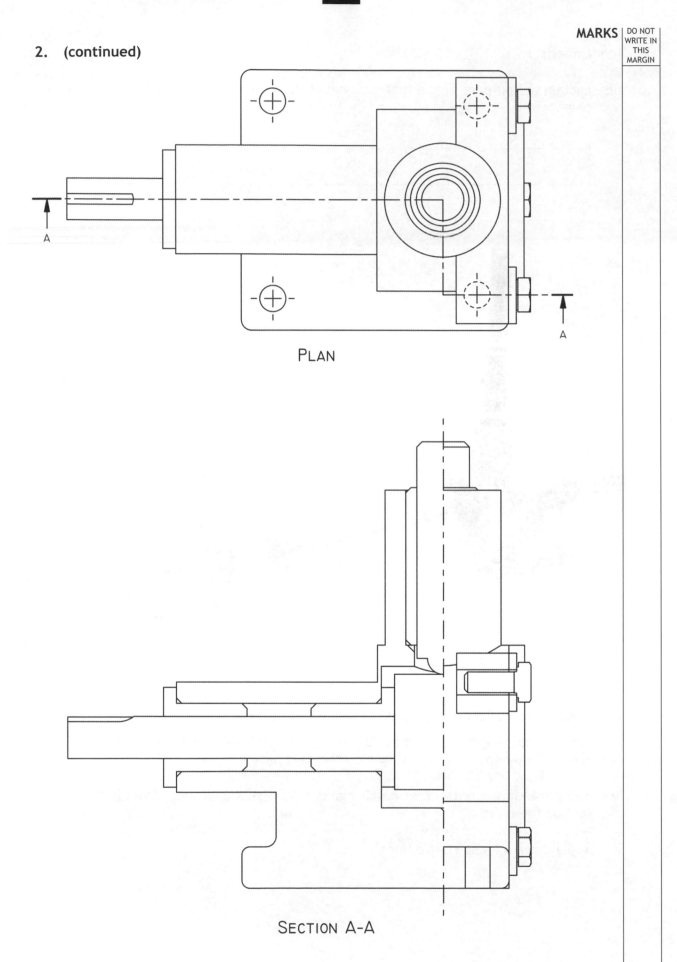

PLAN

SECTION A-A

MARKS | DO NOT WRITE IN THIS MARGIN

3. A new recycling bin with chutes at different heights is being created. It has been designed to introduce young children to the importance of recycling by enabling them to reach the chutes.

The recycle bin comprises four components:

1   The bin prism — a hexagonal prism

2   Two chutes — both hexagonal prisms

3   The lid — another hexagonal prism

Production drawings are being completed to support manufacture. Study the drawings carefully before answering the questions.

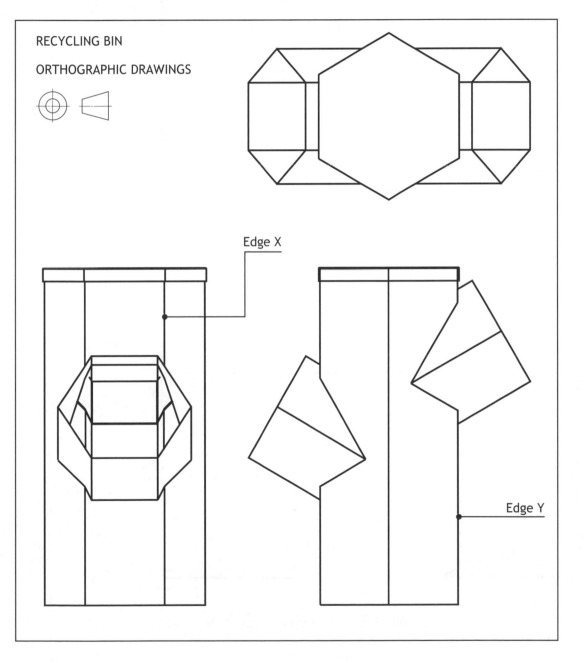

RECYCLING BIN

ORTHOGRAPHIC DRAWINGS

Edge X

Edge Y

MARKS | DO NOT
WRITE IN
THIS
MARGIN

3. **(continued)**

An incomplete surface development of the bin prism is shown. The base and glue tabs have still to be added. The development shows the outside of the bin prism.

i. Identify the fold lines that represent edges X and Y. 2

You should label clearly edge X and edge Y.

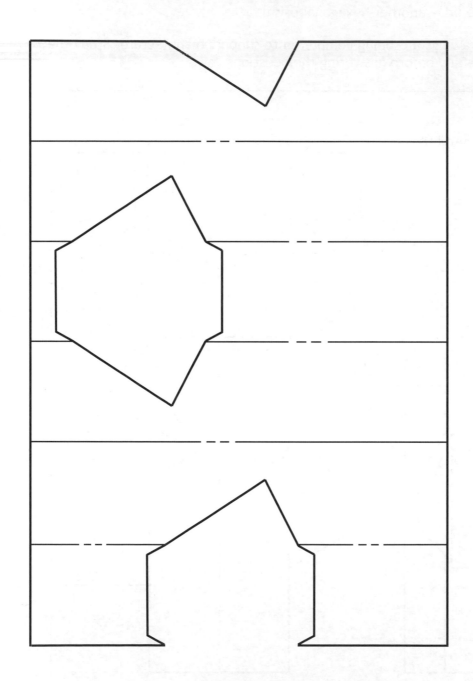

Bin Prism Development External View

MARKS | DO NOT WRITE IN THIS MARGIN

3. **(continued)**

The illustration below shows the final colour scheme and graphics applied to the bins. The graphics comprise the two lines of text "RECYCLING" and "IS FUN" as well as two yellow horizontal stripes and one pattern of yellow circles.

ii. Identify where the graphics and text should be placed on the surface development.

Add them to the surface development on the previous page.

Ensure you estimate the position and orientation of the graphics accurately.

2

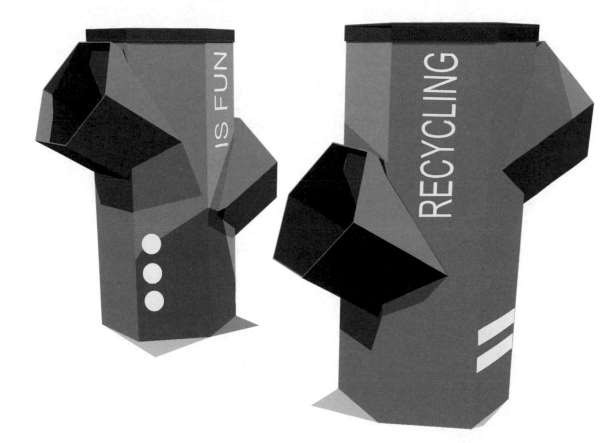

MARKS | DO NOT WRITE IN THIS MARGIN

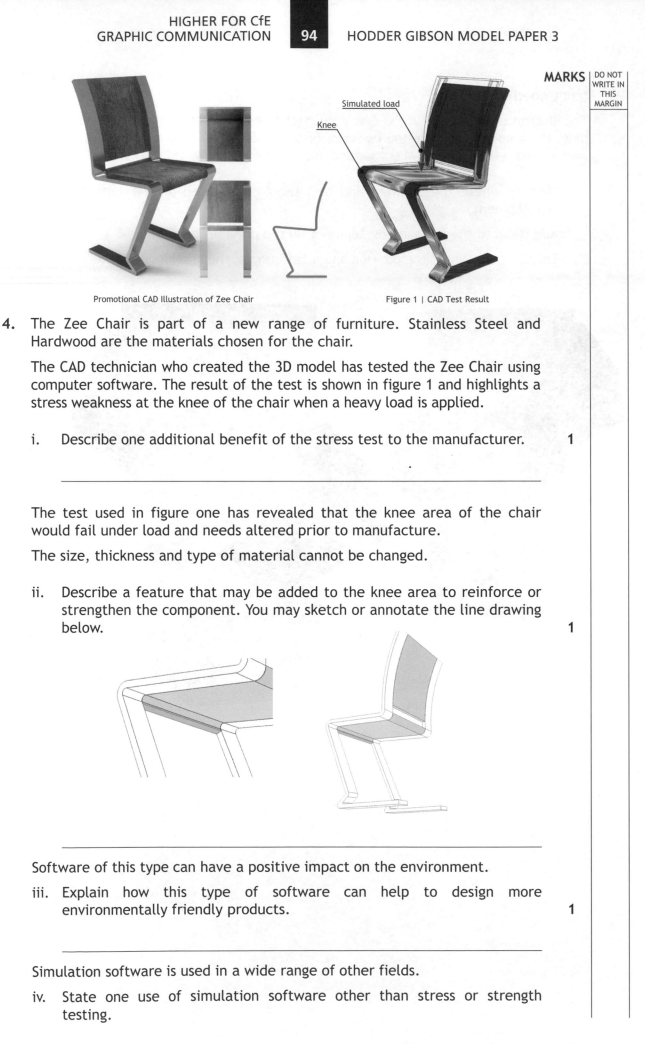

Promotional CAD Illustration of Zee Chair   Figure 1 | CAD Test Result

4. The Zee Chair is part of a new range of furniture. Stainless Steel and Hardwood are the materials chosen for the chair.

The CAD technician who created the 3D model has tested the Zee Chair using computer software. The result of the test is shown in figure 1 and highlights a stress weakness at the knee of the chair when a heavy load is applied.

i.   Describe one additional benefit of the stress test to the manufacturer.   1

The test used in figure one has revealed that the knee area of the chair would fail under load and needs altered prior to manufacture.

The size, thickness and type of material cannot be changed.

ii. Describe a feature that may be added to the knee area to reinforce or strengthen the component. You may sketch or annotate the line drawing below.   1

Software of this type can have a positive impact on the environment.

iii. Explain how this type of software can help to design more environmentally friendly products.   1

Simulation software is used in a wide range of other fields.

iv. State one use of simulation software other than stress or strength testing.

1

MARKS | DO NOT WRITE IN THIS MARGIN

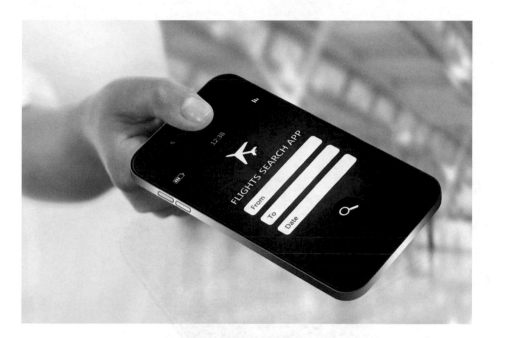

5. A low budget airline is trying to attract more business by improving the customer experience of searching and booking flights. As part of their plan, they have created an "app" for smartphones.

    i. Describe two challenges the graphic designer would face when creating the user interface for the app.   2

    _____

    _____

    The airline would like to encourage customers to book hotels through their app so they can charge a commission.

    Hotels that would like to work with the airline are asked to send in their logo and images of their hotel to be displayed through the app. The airline is requesting "thumbnail" size images to be used only.

    ii. Explain why the airline would request thumbnail size images.   2

    _____

    _____

    The airline operates in many countries around the world and would like users of the app to be able to change the language settings easily using a visual method requiring no words.

    iii. Describe a graphical solution to allow users to select the language the app is displayed in.   1

    _____

    _____

5.   (continued)

The airline are wanting to reduce costs and waste by not printing boarding passes. They are encouraging customers to use the app as the boarding pass for their flights.

The app will display a "QR" image that airport staff can scan to allow customers on board their flight.

iv.   Describe two issues that the passenger and airport may encounter by customers using the app as a boarding pass.

2

_____

_____

6.

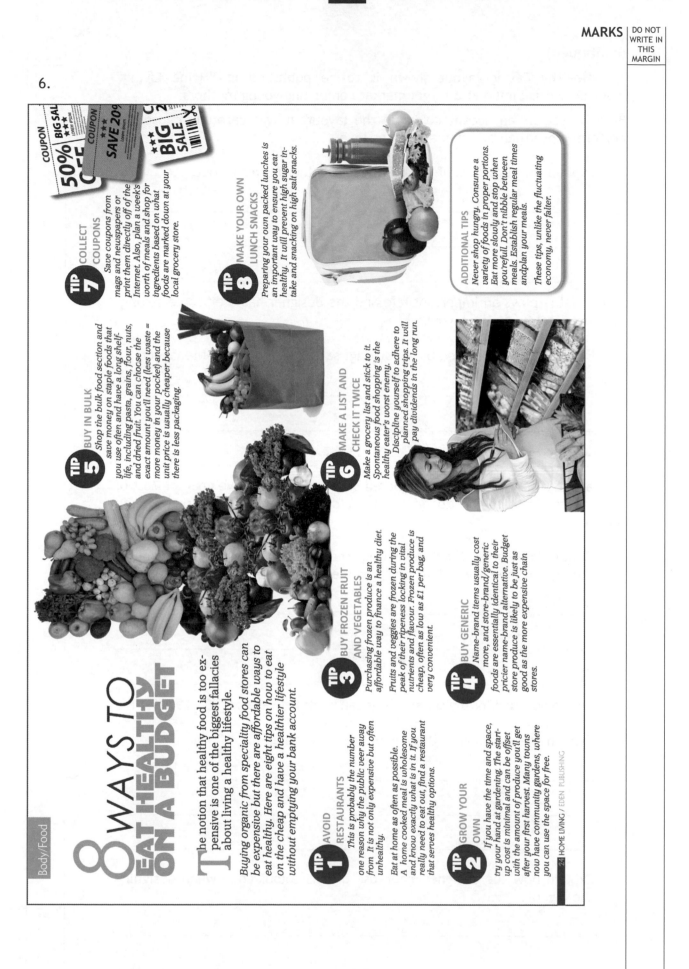

Body/Food

8 WAYS TO EAT HEALTHY ON A BUDGET

The notion that healthy food is too expensive is one of the biggest fallacies about living a healthy lifestyle.

Buying organic from speciality food stores can be expensive but there are affordable ways to eat healthy. Here are eight tips on how to eat on the cheap and have a healthier lifestyle without emptying your bank account.

TIP 1 AVOID RESTAURANTS

This is probably the number one reason why the public veer away from. It is not only expensive but often unhealthy.

Eat at home as often as possible. A home cooked meal is wholesome and know exactly what is in it. If you really need to eat out, find a restaurant that serves healthy options.

TIP 2 GROW YOUR OWN

If you have the time and space, try your hand at gardening. The start-up cost is minimal and can be offset with the amount of produce you'll get after your first harvest. Many towns now have community gardens, where you can use the space for free.

TIP 3 BUY FROZEN FRUIT AND VEGETABLES

Purchasing frozen produce is an affordable way to finance a healthy diet.

Fruits and veggies are frozen during the peak of their ripeness locking in vital nutrients and flavour. Frozen produce is cheap, often as low as £1 per bag, and very convenient.

TIP 4 BUY GENERIC

Name-brand items usually cost more, and store-brand/generic foods are essentially identical to their pricier name-brand alternative. Budget store produce is likely to be just as good as the more expensive chain stores.

TIP 5 BUY IN BULK

Shop the bulk food section and save money on staple foods that you use often and have a long shelf life, including pasta, grains, flour, nuts, and dried fruit. You can choose the exact amount you'll need (less waste = more money in your pocket) and the unit price is usually cheaper because there is less packaging.

TIP 6 MAKE A LIST AND CHECK IT TWICE

Make a grocery list and stick to it. Spontaneous food shopping is the healthy eater's worst enemy.

Discipline yourself to adhere to planned shopping trips. It will pay dividends in the long run.

TIP 7 COLLECT COUPONS

Save coupons from mags and newspapers or print them directly off of the Internet. Also, plan a week's worth of meals and shop for ingredients based on what foods are marked down at your local grocery store.

TIP 8 MAKE YOUR OWN LUNCH SNACKS

Preparing your own packed lunches is an important way to ensure you eat healthy. It will prevent high sugar in-take and snacking on high salt snacks.

ADDITIONAL TIPS

Never shop hungry. Consume a variety of foods in proper portions. Eat more slowly and stop when you're full. Don't nibble between meals. Establish regular meal times and plan your meals.

These tips, unlike the fluctuating economy, never falter.

24 HOME LIVING / EDEN PUBLISHING

MARKS | DO NOT WRITE IN THIS MARGIN

6. **(continued)**

The Healthy Eating layout shown is to be published in "Home Living" magazine. It is aimed at a target market comprising young mothers.

Blue is used as an accent colour in the layout. It was carefully chosen to perform more than one function in the layout.

i.   Explain the functions of the blue accent colour in this layout.   2

_____

_____

_____

Colour value plays an important role and the designer has used some **strong**, **saturated colour** in the layout.

ii. Explain the roles played by the **strong**, **saturated colour** in the layout.   2

_____

_____

_____

The layout is busy with eleven numbered blocks of text and five images. Most of the images relate to the tips given. It could easily become confusing for the reader.

iii. Explain how, other than numbering, the designer made it easy to follow the layout and easy to interpret the messages given in the layout.   3

_____

_____

_____

The blue colour used for the sub-headings can be described as: C 70, M 9, Y 2, K 0

iv. Explain the meaning of this colour coding system.   2

_____

_____

_____

v.   Explain how the designer made use of this colour code when designing the layout.   2

_____

_____

_____

MARKS | DO NOT WRITE IN THIS MARGIN

6.   (continued)

The blocks of text are arranged in columns but the images in the layout are placed outside the column structure.

vi.   Explain why the images have been placed outwith the column structure.   **2**

_____

_____

_____

The text in the layout is divided into a 5 level hierarchy (order) of importance that takes the following order:

1. Title, 2. Main Sub-Heading, 3. Sub-Headings, 4. Body text, 5. Header and footer.

The graphic designer used several DTP techniques to ensure that the title, below, is the dominant text in the layout. Choice of typeface, colours, font size and the use of kerning are four DTP techniques the designer used to create impact in the title.

8 WAYS TO
EAT HEALTHY
ON A BUDGET

vii.   Describe two other techniques the designer has used to maximise the impact of the title.   **2**

_____

_____

viii.   Kerning was used in the title to create impact.
Explain the term kerning and how it is used to create impact in headings.   **2**

_____

_____

MARKS | DO NOT WRITE IN THIS MARGIN

6. (continued)

An earlier design for the title is shown on the right.

ix. Explain why this design does not work as well as the one used in the layout.   **3**

_____

_____

_____

The designer used a serif typeface for the body text.

x. Explain the term serif typeface.
You may sketch and annotate your answer.   **1**

_____

_____

_____

xi. Justify the designer's choice of a serif typeface for the body text. (Give two reasons in your answer.)   **2**

_____

_____

_____

The layout was created using DTP software and was converted to a PDF file.

xii. Explain why the file was converted to a PDF.   **1**

_____

_____

_____

MARKS | DO NOT WRITE IN THIS MARGIN

6.   (continued)

An alternative layout, below, makes use of a pull quote.

xiii. Explain one function of a pull quote.   1

_____

_____

_____

_____

_____

[END OF MODEL PAPER]

H

National
Qualifications
2015

Mark

X735/76/01

Graphic Communication

THURSDAY, 30 APRIL
1:00 PM – 3:00 PM

Fill in these boxes and read what is printed below.

Full name of centre

Town

Forename(s)

Surname

Number of seat

Date of birth

Day	Month	Year	Scottish candidate number

Total marks — 70

Attempt ALL questions.

All dimensions are in mm.

All technical sketches and drawings use third angle projection.

You may use rulers, compasses or trammels for measuring.

In all questions you may use sketches and annotations to support your answer if you wish.

Write your answers clearly in the spaces provided in this booklet. Additional space for answers is provided at the end of this booklet. If you use this space you must clearly identify the question number you are attempting.

Use **blue** or **black** ink.

Before leaving the examination room you must give this booklet to the Invigilator; if you do not, you may lose all the marks for this paper.

[BLANK PAGE]

DO NOT WRITE ON THIS PAGE

MARKS | DO NOT WRITE IN THIS MARGIN

Total marks — 70

Attempt ALL questions

1. A CAD Technician created a 3D model of the fire extinguisher, shown below.

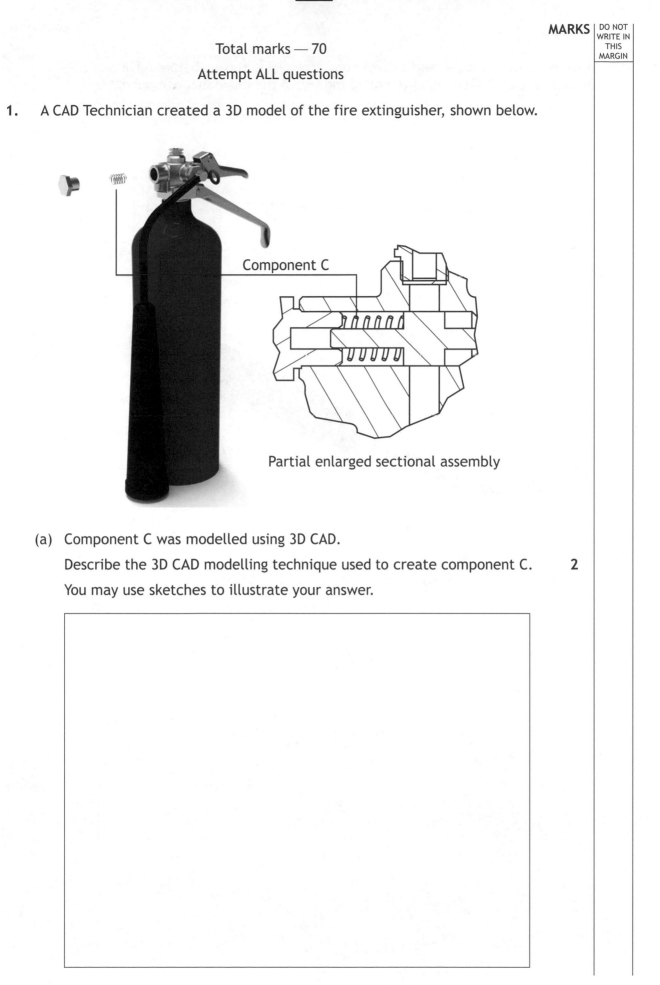

Component C

Partial enlarged sectional assembly

(a) Component C was modelled using 3D CAD.

Describe the 3D CAD modelling technique used to create component C.   2

You may use sketches to illustrate your answer.

[Turn over

1. (continued)

A drawing of the pipe and nozzle sub-assembly is shown below. This was used by the CAD Technician to create models of the individual components.

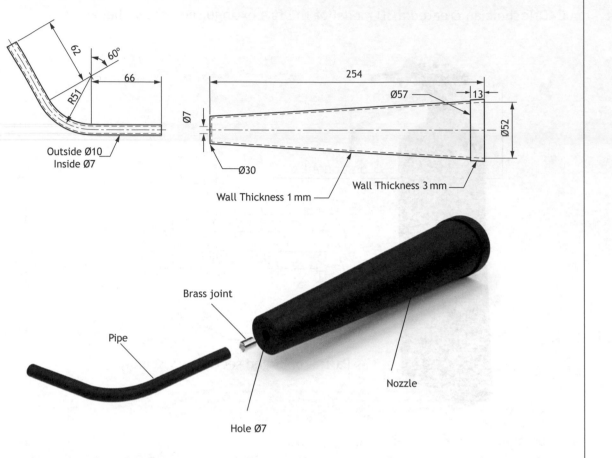

(b) Describe the 3D CAD modelling techniques used to create the **pipe** component. Refer to the dimensions given in the drawing.   **3**

MARKS | DO NOT WRITE IN THIS MARGIN

1. (continued)

(c) Describe the 3D CAD modelling techniques used to create the **nozzle** component. Refer to the dimensions given in the drawing.

6

[Turn over

1. (continued)

The manufacturer of the fire extinguisher would like to provide a simple wall bracket to hold their product.

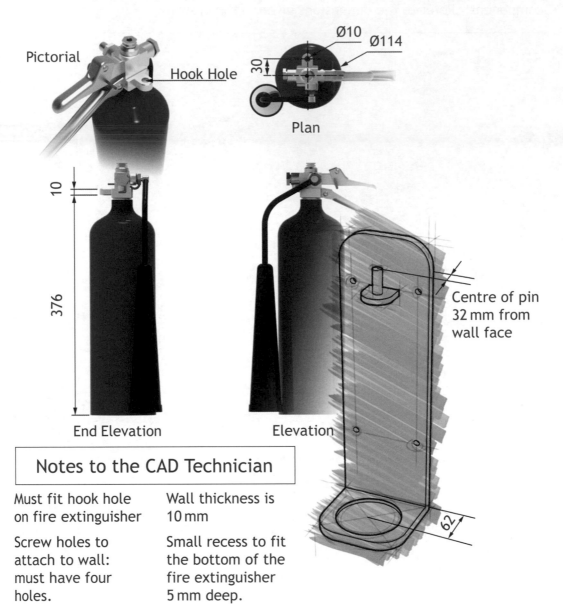

Pictorial

Hook Hole

Ø10   Ø114

30

Plan

10

376

End Elevation

Elevation

Centre of pin
32 mm from
wall face

62

Notes to the CAD Technician

Must fit hook hole on fire extinguisher

Screw holes to attach to wall: must have four holes.

Wall thickness is 10 mm

Small recess to fit the bottom of the fire extinguisher 5 mm deep.

MARKS | DO NOT WRITE IN THIS MARGIN

1. **(continued)**

    (d) Describe the 3D CAD modelling techniques used to create the wall bracket.

    Use measurements from the rendered orthographic and the "Notes to the CAD Technician". You may use sketches to explain your answer.

    7

2. Glasgow Riverside Museum opened in 2011. As with any other building built in this country the architecture firm was required to submit a number of different drawings to the local authority to gain planning permission. During this process the architects also produced a number of other graphics for different purposes.

Figure 1

Figure 2

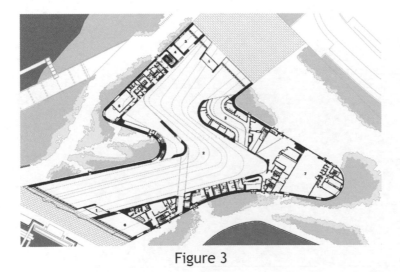

Figure 3

MARKS | DO NOT WRITE IN THIS MARGIN

2. (continued)

(a) **Explain**, with reference to the 3P's, the purpose of each of the graphics shown in Figures 1, 2 and 3.   3

The scales commonly used for figure 3 are 1:50 or 1:100.

(b) State **two** factors that influence the choice of scale in this type of graphic.   2

[Turn over

MARKS | DO NOT WRITE IN THIS MARGIN

2. (continued)

Sectional views are commonly used in the construction industry.
Cross-hatching is a feature found in sectional construction views.

(c) Describe the benefits of applying cross-hatching to a sectional
     construction drawing.   2

The standardised construction drawing symbols and conventions shown
below are commonly found in many construction drawings.

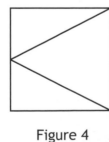

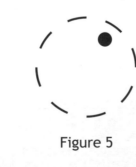

Figure 4   Figure 5   Figure 6

(d) **Identify** each of the symbols/conventions.   3

     Figure 4 _____

     Figure 5 _____

     Figure 6 _____

MARKS | DO NOT WRITE IN THIS MARGIN

3. With the rise in popularity of tablets and smartphones, publishers now produce most of their publications in both hardcopy and digital versions.

(a) **Describe** the advantages to the consumer that the digital format offers over the hardcopy.

2

(b) **Describe** why companies advertising within the publication may prefer the digital format to the hardcopy format.

2

3.   (continued)

Some publishers are considering moving completely to a digital based distribution of their publications.

(c)   **Explain** the disadvantages in the distribution of the digital version over the hardcopy version.

4

[Turn over for Question 4 on *page fourteen*

DO NOT WRITE ON THIS PAGE

MARKS

4. A furniture designer has produced a 3D CAD illustration of a new table design. The furniture designer needs to prepare the design for manufacture.

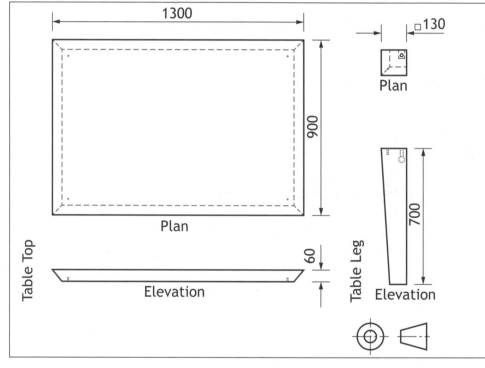

Figure 1

The component drawing of the table top and legs, in Figure 1, are drawn to a scale.

(a) Measure and calculate the scale used for Figure 1.   1

MARKS

4. (continued)

The manufacturer has recommended that tolerances be applied to components of the table. They have suggested the following tolerances;

Length of table leg +1·5mm and –0·5mm

Thickness of table top +2·5 mm and –1·5mm

(b) Calculate the maximum and minimum allowable heights of the fully assembled table after applying the tolerances.

    2

    Maximum height _____ mm   Minimum height _____ mm

(c) Apply the dimensional tolerances to the views below using the correct British Standard conventions.

    2

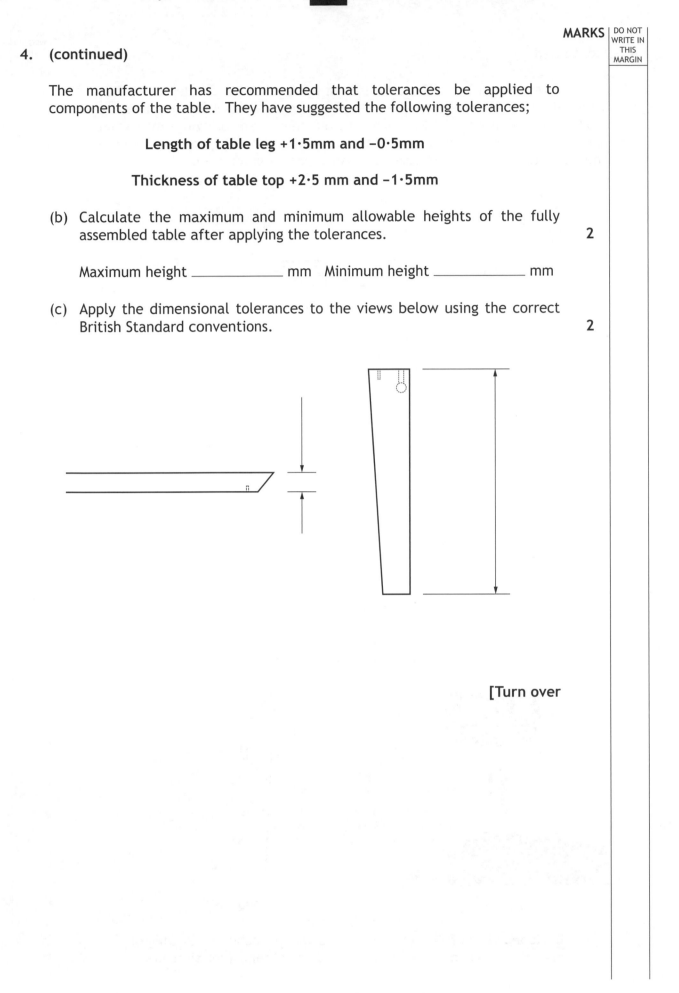

[Turn over

MARKS | DO NOT WRITE IN THIS MARGIN

4.   (continued)

Knock-down fittings are commonly used in flat-pack furniture design as they make furniture easy to assemble; they require no specialist skills and are easily mass produced. Shown below are the component drawings for two of the most common knock-down fittings used by the retailer (figures 2 and 3) and extracts from the draft assembly instructions (figures 4 and 5).

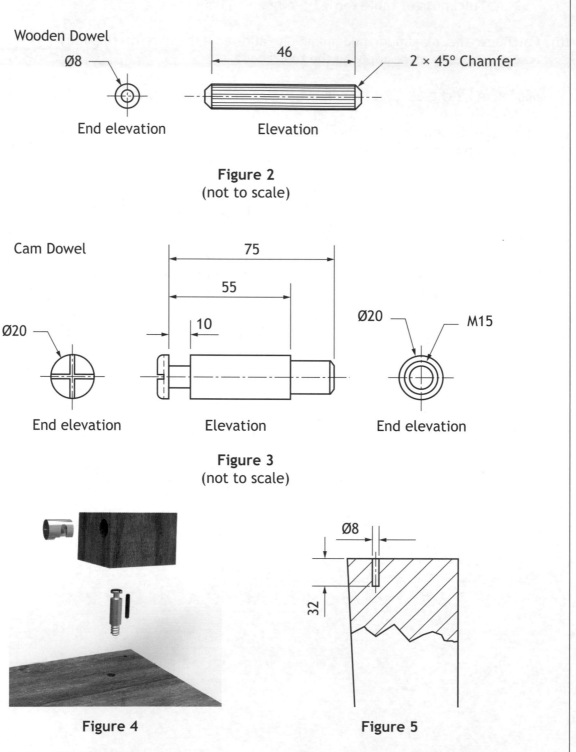

Wooden Dowel

Ø8

46

2 × 45° Chamfer

End elevation   Elevation

Figure 2
(not to scale)

Cam Dowel

75

55

10

Ø20   Ø20   M15

End elevation   Elevation   End elevation

Figure 3
(not to scale)

Ø8

32

Figure 4

Exploded view of
assembly method

Figure 5

Enlarged technical drawing of
dowel joint (not to scale)

MARKS | DO NOT WRITE IN THIS MARGIN

4. **(continued)**

The component drawing for the Cam Dowel is incomplete.

(d) Apply the British Standard conventions for the screw threads in each view in Figure 6 below.   **2**

Figure 6

In preparation for manufacture of the table top, the furniture designer has been asked to specify some measurements.

(e) Calculate how far the wooden dowel protrudes from the table leg when fully inserted.   **1**

_____ mm

(f) Calculate the minimum depth of hole required to be drilled in the table top to accommodate the Cam Dowel.   **1**

_____ mm

(g) State the type of linear dimensioning used in the elevation view of the Cam Dowel in Figure 3.   **1**

_____

(h) State the type of the sectional view in Figure 5.   **1**

_____

[Turn over

MARKS | DO NOT WRITE IN THIS MARGIN

5. Study the magazine pages, read the judges' comments carefully and answer the following questions.

The double page layouts in the magazines have each won graphic design awards.

Below each layout is a comment made by the judges about the success of the layout.

(a)

Judges' comments

"Be yourself – you can't be anyone else", an interview with Kelly Osbourne, takes a dynamic image and combines it with the interview in a simple but effective way. The connection with the young female target market is strong and the use of typeface is creative".

Describe how the designer has used the **headline** to **connect with a target audience** and to **create visual contrast**.

4

5. (continued)

MARKS | DO NOT WRITE IN THIS MARGIN

(b)

Judges' comments

"The windsurfing layout captures the excitement of the sport while showing a strongly unified layout across both pages. It uses techniques that connect with its young, sporty target audience."

(i)   Explain the ways in which the designer has used DTP techniques to create **unity** in the layout.

2

(ii)   Describe how the designer used DTP features to introduce **proportion** in the layout.

2

5. (continued)

(c)

Judges' comments

"The article about T.I. the American rapper and producer, demonstrates clever use of space. The graphic designer took a photograph which oozes attitude and created a clean and modern layout around it. Also, the designer used several clever and subtle tricks to create contrast and visual impact".

The graphic designer uses **DTP features** to incorporate **shape** in the layout.

Explain how the designer's use of shape improves the layout.

3

MARKS | DO NOT WRITE IN THIS MARGIN

6. A review of music festivals was commissioned by "NEWmusic" magazine. The magazine's readers are in the 18-28 years age range. The musical styles covered by the magazine are "indie" and "rock".

   Use the two layouts in the **supplementary sheet for use with Question 6** provided to answer this question.

   A graphic designer submitted version 1 of his festival review for consideration but this was not accepted for publication. Version 2 was then developed and was published in "NEWmusic" magazine.

   The following questions require you to compare how the designer has applied **design elements** and **principles** in each of the versions and describe the impact they have on the layouts.

   Colour is a feature in both layouts

   (a) Compare the use of **colour** in the layouts.   2

   Alignment is a consideration whenever a layout is created.

   (b) Compare the use of **alignment** in both layouts.   4

MARKS | DO NOT WRITE IN THIS MARGIN

6.   (continued)

Designers choose a style of **balance** to suit the purpose of the layout.

(c)   Compare the use of **balance** in both layouts.   2

Texture can be an important visual feature in a layout.

(d)   Compare the use of **texture** in both layouts.   2

Graphic designers use **emphasis** for a number of purposes.

(e)   Compare the use of **emphasis** in both layouts.   2

[END OF QUESTION PAPER]

ADDITIONAL SPACE FOR ANSWERS

ADDITIONAL SPACE FOR ANSWERS

MARKS | DO NOT WRITE IN THIS MARGIN

[BLANK PAGE]

DO NOT WRITE ON THIS PAGE

[BLANK PAGE]

DO NOT WRITE ON THIS PAGE

[BLANK PAGE]

DO NOT WRITE ON THIS PAGE

National
Qualifications
2015

X735/76/11

**Graphic Communication
Supplementary Sheet**

THURSDAY, 30 APRIL

1:00 PM – 3:00 PM

Supplementary sheet for use with Question 6

Supplementary sheet for use with Question 6

Festivals
2013

UTunes

The UTunes Festival. 30 days of live music from the biggest bands and artists. This jam-packed festival ranged from bands such as Kings of Leon to artists such as Avicii. For anybody who enjoys seeing all of the big bands this is the festival to go to.

Blastin Merry

Dziurek/Shutterstock.com

Blastin' Merry 2013 sure was a festival to relish. Artists such as Example, Chase and Status, the Rolling Stones, Mumford and Sons and many more contributed to the extremely action packed, enjoyable Festival that everyone seems to know and love. The Rolling Stones made the most impact on festival goers and people of all ages enjoyed their music.

R&R on the Farm

From Headliners such as Rihanna, Mumford and Sons to Jake Bugg and Alt-J, R&R on the Farm made it big this year. A year in which 'R&R' celebrated its 20th anniversary as the biggest and perhaps best Scottish music festival.

Fans were treated to nice weather too which made a welcome and well deserved change to the weather conditions at recent festivals. It all added up to make Galado a magical place for the entire weekend.

Christian Bertrand/Shutterstock.com

Festivals 2013

R&R on the Farm

From Headliners such as Rihanna, Mumford and Sons to Jake Bugg and Alt-J, R&R on the Farm made it big this year. A year in which 'R&R' celebrated its 20th anniversary as the biggest and perhaps best Scottish music festival. Fans were treated to nice weather too which made a welcome and well deserved change to the weather conditions at recent festivals. It all added up to make Galado a magical place for the entire weekend.

Christian Bertrand/Shutterstock.com

Blastin' Merry

Blastin' Merry 2013 sure was a festival to relish. Artists such as Example, Chase and Status, the Rolling Stones, Mumford and Sons and many more contributed to the extremely action packed, enjoyable Festival that everyone seems to know and love. The Rolling Stones made the most impact on festival goers and people of all ages enjoyed their music.

Dziurek/Shutterstock.com

UTunes

The UTunes Festival. 30 days of live music from the biggest bands and artists. This jam-packed festival ranged from bands such as Kings of Leon to artists such as Avicii. For anybody who enjoys seeing almost all of the big bands this is the festival to go to.

[BLANK PAGE]

DO NOT WRITE ON THIS PAGE

SQA AND HODDER GIBSON HIGHER FOR CfE GRAPHIC COMMUNICATION 2015

General Marking Principles for Higher Graphic Communication

Questions that ask candidates to "describe"

Candidates must provide a statement or structure of characteristics and/or features. This should be more than an outline or a list. Candidates may refer to, for instance, a concept, experiment, situation, or facts in the context of and appropriate to the question. Candidates will normally be required to make the same number of factual/appropriate points as are awarded in the question.

Questions that ask candidates to "explain"

Candidates must generally relate cause and effect and/or make relationships between things clear. These will be related to the context of the question or a specific area within a question.

Questions that ask candidates to "compare"

Candidates must generally demonstrate knowledge and understanding of the similarities and/or differences between, for instance, things, methods, or choices. These will be related to the context of the question or a specific area within a question.

Candidates can respond to any question using text, sketching, annotations or combinations where they prefer. No marks shall be awarded for the quality of sketching. Marking will relate only to the information being conveyed.

HIGHER FOR CfE GRAPHIC COMMUNICATION SPECIMEN QUESTION PAPER

Question			Expected response	Max mark
1.	(a)	(i)	**Re-drawing** Advantages can cover: • option to add in layers • easy to edit/modify • can use in simulations • produces vector graphic • small file size • updated drawings to include modern drawing standards or any other appropriate response. Disadvantages can cover: • very time consuming • mistakes could be made or any other appropriate response. **Scanning** Advantages can cover: • speed • file can be archived • file can be emailed • files are easily viewed on many electronic devices or any other appropriate response. Disadvantages can cover: • drawings cannot be edited after scanning • file sizes • produces raster graphic • physical drawing sizes may prove too large to scan in one attempt (may require piecing together) or any other appropriate advantage/disadvantage.	4
		(ii)	Any relevant explanation made regarding: • the incompatibility of file types • drawing standards • files cannot be worked on simultaneously by different parties • possible complications in language barriers	2

Question			Expected response	Max mark
	(b)		Any appropriate and specific aspect for testing such as: • heat flow • flow of people (dynamic) • static loading • strength of material • ventilation flow/rate • light • evacuation time	1
	(c)		Any appropriate advantage such as: • ease of storage • ease of sharing • ease of collaborative working • positive environmental aspects • reduction in copying or any other appropriate advantage.	1
2.	(a)	(i)	Description which makes reference to: • the loft command to join profiles (1 mark) **and** • the size of the profiles (40 mm x 40 mm) **and** a distance of 120 mm (1 mark)	2
		(ii)	Description which makes reference to: • extruding a cuboid 40 mm and applying a radius to the end edges (1 mark) **and** • drawing a profile on the end of the 3D model, 40 mm x 40 mm (1 mark) **OR** • extruding the profile 40 mm (1 mark) **and** • drawing a profile the shape indicated on the sketch (1 mark)	2

Question			Expected response	Max mark
	(b)		A description which makes reference to: • using the shell solid command to remove interior material from the solid model (1 mark) **and** • creating a sketch through the solid model (lengthways). The sketch must be bigger than the solid model (1 mark) **and** • extruding the sketch with a subtraction in one direction and saving the file (1 mark) **and** • redefining the modelling tree/ extrusion and subtract in the opposite direction and saving the file under a different name (1 mark) **OR** • creating a sketch through the solid model (lengthways) — the sketch must be bigger than the solid model (1 mark) **and** • extruding the sketch with a subtraction in one direction (1 mark) **and** • using the shell command to remove a face and hollow the model and then saving the file (1 mark) **and** • redefining the modelling tree/ extrusion and subtract in the opposite direction and saving the file under a different name (1 mark) or any other suitable **top down** approach in the **correct order.**	4
	(c)		An explanation of the appropriateness of inclusion of the item such as: • removes repetition • saves time on drawing common or complex components • common components in a CAD library are likely to conform to standards • accurately represent common or frequently used parts • library components can be used or shared between a wide range of models • library components can be used or shared between a wide range of technicians, operators or people or any other appropriate explanation.	2

Question			Expected response	Max mark
	(d)		An outline description which makes reference to constraining methods, eg: • centre the axis of two corresponding screw-bosses or centre the axis of the two corresponding radiused case components (1 mark) **and** • mate the two flat faces on the components, either on the outer case or the bosses (1 mark) **OR** any other appropriate description.	2
	(e)		Production of a modelling plan which communicates how **key** features of the 3D model are generated in relation to the criteria of the question. Responses should include references to: • 140 mm between centres (1 mark) • minimum 30 mm clearance for handle (1 mark) • 10 mm diameter for the handle (1 mark) • any suitable modelling technique to complete the handle (1 mark) or within any other workable modelling plan.	4
3.			Explanations should make appropriate reference to (and relate the choices made to): • Target market (consumer) • o families • o hygiene aware • o families with young children • Colour scheme/choice of images • o fresh • o hygienic • o calm • o natural • o health • o safety • o link to broccoli (fresh, organic, natural) • Typeface • o sans serif font • o modern • o use of product logo to promote brand • o use of uppercase to emphasise the bio/eco aspect of the product or any other appropriate description.	4

Question			Expected response	Max mark
4.	(a)	(i)		3
		(ii)	Web	1
		(iii)		1
	(b)	(i)		2
		(ii)	A blind hole is a hole that is drilled or milled to a specified depth without breaking through to the other side of the material.	1
		(iii)	Metric	1
		(iv)	30 mm	1
		(v)	Local or part section	1

Question			Expected response	Max mark
		(vi)		1
5.	(a)			2

Generator line	Offset from line X (mm) (within the ranges)
1	13—15
2	18·5—20·5
3	27·5—29·5
4	37·5—39·5
5	37—39
6	37·5—39·5
7	36·5—38·5
Circle centre point	17—19

Question			Expected response	Max mark
	(b)		Candidate's response must be within the following ranges: X = 57—58 mm Z = 49—51 mm	1
6.	(a)		Explanations such as: • The serif fonts are formal, traditional or old fashioned. • They represent a more sophisticated or mature look to appeal to the older target market. • The flicks and flowing curves in the font styles look friendly and safe to an older target market. • Each letter flowing into the next makes it easier for an older target market to read. Or any other appropriate explanation.	2

Question		Expected response	Max mark
(b)		Explanations such as: • The page is rectilinear and so are the boxes, lines and the square. • The cropped images create curved or natural shapes that bring eye-catching contrast with/visual interest against the rectilinear shapes. • The cropped cyclist and helmet (the product) stand out against a simple geometric backdrop. • The punctuation circles add contrast against the rectilinear shapes in the layout. **OR** • The curved text above the cyclist creates contrast with the rectilinear shapes in the layout. • The purpose of the advert is to attract attention quickly; the contrasting shapes (mentioned earlier) help ensure this. • The curved text mimics (harmonises with) the shape of the helmet and appears to protect the cyclist's head. Or any other appropriate explanation.	2
(c)		Explanations such as: The orange line: • creates a unifying accent colour with the other orange items • creates depth by passing behind the cyclist • underlines (emphasises) part of the slogan The blue vertical line: • creates depth by passing behind the helmet • creates eye-catching contrast with the horizontal lines • harmonises with the horizontal blue line • separates the space for the web address The blue horizontal line: • connects the layout items horizontally • aids alignment with the slogan and company name • creates eye-catching contrast with the orange colours • harmonises with the vertical blue line • creates a vertical/horizontal contrast • separates the space for the company name or any other appropriate explanation.	3

Question		Expected response	Max mark
(d)		The advancing colour is red or orange. A description such as: The effect this colour has on the layout is that: • it lifts the red or orange items forward • makes the red or orange items more prominent • makes the red or orange items stand out more • creates contrast with the receding colours in the layout or any other appropriate description.	2
(e)	(i)	An explanation such as: • it leaves two awkward spaces to fill rather than one usable space/ it misses the most natural focal points. or any other appropriate explanation.	1
	(ii)	An explanation such as: • it will create visual interest through asymmetry, white space, and a natural focal point. • it leaves a single space that is easier to fill/populate. or any other appropriate explanation.	1
6. (f)		An explanation such as: • The font is a graffiti/grungy/sans serif style and is fun and youthful. • Images of mountain bike stunts connect with target market. • Tilted images and items make the layout less formal and create visual interest. • Bold, contrasting colours (blue and red) create a youthful look. • Distressed images will appeal to young target market. Or any other appropriate explanation.	3
7. (a)		Explanation for headers and footers such as: • They can assist in navigating within a document. • They display useful information including, title/chapter, page number, date, author. • They identify the document's content. • They create a sense of unity throughout a document or section.	2
(b)	(i)	Crop marks	1
	(ii)	Explanation such as: • Crop marks illustrate the boundary where the document is to be cut after printing.	1

Question		Expected response	Max mark
	(iii)	Explanation such as: • To bleed is to extend a graphic or image frame beyond a trimmed edge of the page. • To ensure the graphic or image extends to the very edge of the page of a document. • Edge to edge printing.	1
(c)		Description of layering such as: • Layering can support in creating a master page for future documents. • Layering allows graphics and text to be edited separately. • Layering supports image manipulation and can occur on separate layers. • Layers can be duplicated and linked to other layers. • Layers can be turned off or on to aid clarity. • Layers can be brought forward or backward as necessary.	2
(d)	(i)	Explanation of impact of use of reverse such as: • offsets the main text from the headline/sub-headline • lightens the layout (decreases the value)	2
	(ii)	Explanation of impact of dropped capital such as: • emphasises the start of a paragraph • signifies the main text column	2
	(iii)	Explanation of impact of when the main text column is converted from one to two columns such as: • follows a standard method of presenting a main body of text • assists with the readability of the document	2

HIGHER FOR CfE GRAPHIC COMMUNICATION MODEL PAPER 1

Question		Comments	Marks
1	(i)	• Create a rectangular profile that intersects the water pistol along the length. • Extrude subtract in one direction and save file. • Edit modelling tree to extrude subtract in the opposite direction and Save-As file.	3
	(ii)		7
	(iii)		7
	(iv)	• Create a circle of DIA 6mm and create a circle of DIA 4mm, concentric with first circle. • Create a sketch path of 150mm length, rising 20mm. • Extrude along a path.	3

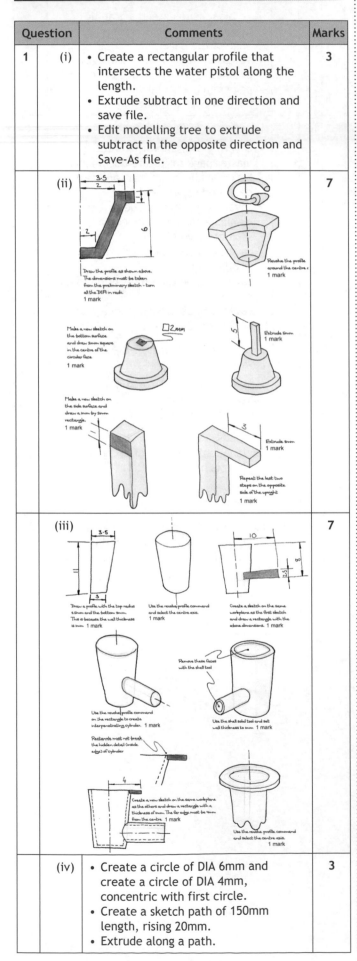

Question		Comments	Marks
	(v)	CADCAM Computer Aided Design Computer Aided Manufacture	1
	(vi)	• Physical models allow people to appreciate the proportions of a particular item. • Physical models can be used to test particular features. • Physical models cannot be altered easily. • 3D CAD models can be emailed around the world. • 3D CAD models can be illustrated and animated. • 3D CAD models can be used to manufacture the final item. *Any two of the above.*	2
2	(i)	• Three components cross hatched in the right areas (1 mark each). • Correct changes of direction of cross-hatching (1 mark). • Correct staggering of cross hatching (1 mark). • No cross-hatching on any other areas (1 mark). (Answers can be explained or sketched or a combination of both).	6
	(ii)	Overall assembled length is 7536.	1
	(iii)	It is used to indicate that the object has been shortened to fit on the page. It is called a break line and the view it creates is an interrupted view *1 mark for either answer.*	1

Question		Comments	Marks
	(iv)	*Any two from the following for two marks each.*	4
		Graphical Method used to clarify the assembly details: *Exploded views.* Benefits of using this method: *Shows exactly how the parts line up ready for assembly.*	
		Graphical Method used to clarify the assembly details: *Enlarged views.* Benefits of using this method: *Gives a clear, scaled up, picture of small assy details.*	
		Graphical Method used to clarify the assembly details: *Illustrations* Benefits of using this method: *It is more easily understood by non-technical people. It is less complicated to understand.*	
		Graphical Method used to clarify the assembly details: *Sectional views.* Benefits of using this method: *Shows the assembly details that cannot normally be seen.*	
		Graphical Method used to clarify the assembly details: *Interrupted views.* Benefits of using this method: *Enables large or scaled-up drawings to fit on the page.*	
		Graphical Method used to clarify the assembly details: *Dimensioned drawings* Benefits of using this method: *Allows the user to check and compare sizes when assembling the greenhouse.*	
		Acceptable: *orthographic* (showing true faces or sizes) *or pictorial drawings* (easier for the less technical user to understand) with a correct explanation of their benefits.	
	(v)	LEFT END ELEVATION is view 5 RIGHT END ELEVATION is view 8	2
	(vi)	AUXILIARY ELEVATION 1 is view C AUXILIARY ELEVATION 2 is view F	2
	(vii)	The external wall of room 1 that has no window and faces south west.	1

Question		Comments	Marks
	(viii)	The kitchen is planned for room 3. The bathroom is planned for room 5.	2
	(ix)	I identified the kitchen because: It has waste removal plumbing and it has a back door (any one). I identified the bathroom because: It has waste removal plumbing and no outside door (any one). Note: if both answers only refer to the waste removal pipes only one mark is awarded.	2
3	(i)	• Overlapping the layered components (images breaking over the background image etc) using the red underlines to match the red jacket. • The red lines connect the title to the background image. • The red line at the foot connects the background image with the products and the web address. • The body text wraps around the circular image creating unity. *Any two at 1 mark each.*	2
	(ii)	• Increasing the size of the product image, using a drop shadow to bring the images forward. • Using a drop shadow to bring the title forward. • Underlining the title, using layers to position crucial components to the front. • Creating circular and cropped shapes to make the images stand out. *Any two at 1 mark each.*	2
	(iii)	• Creating a circular crop to contrast with the rectangular layout (not enough to state the circle without mentioning how the contrast is achieved). • Using layers to create a near and far (foreground/background) effect. • The use of horizontal lines against a vertical background. *Any two at 1 mark each.*	2
	(iv)	• By creating accurate alignment down the right and the left margins. • The title, sub-head, body text, red line and the bottom and web address are all accurately aligned. • The title, circular image and tent are all accurately aligned right. *Any one of the above.*	1

Question		Comments	Marks
	(v)	The large title is the company name and is the dominant text in the layout. It signals the starting point of the layout. The sub-head sits just below the title and is a smaller font size but larger than the body text. It creates a link between the title and body text. The body text is a smaller font size and is expected to be read after the title and the sub-head. *1 mark for any one and a second mark for describing how the sub-head creates a visual link or bridge etc.*	2
	(vi)	**Title:** The title is a sans serif font in a stylised, distressed style. It has impact required of a heading or title and supports a rugged image compatible with the products and the company's image. (1 mark) **Sub-Head:** The sub-head is in a clean, modern sans serif sized between the title and body text. This creates a link between both title and body text and is suitable for a sound-bite or slogan. (1 mark) **Body text:** The body text is smaller than the others sections and is a serif font. This is more traditional and makes the extended body text easier to read because the serifs help the letters flow. (1 mark)	3
	(vii)	A "bleed" is when an item extends to the edge of the page. A partial "bleed" occurs when only some of the items reach the edge some edges retain a blank margin. *1 mark for each of the above.*	2
	(viii)	By incorporating an active (or positive) image of people who may use the products.	1
	(ix)	The inclusion of a male and a female in the image.	1
4	(i)	By referring to the relationship in the slogans. By showing the natural environment full of bees with the city whose inhabitants depend on bees for food. *1 mark only for referring to the written slogans.*	2
	(ii)	By contrasting the natural environment full of bees in the foreground with the man-made cityscape in the distance. By having the natural environment close up and shown in detail while the cityscape is in the distance *Any one of the above.*	1

Question		Comments	Marks
	(iii)	• Drop shadows create depth. • By establishing a clear foreground (flower and field) and a distant cityscape. • The cropped flower in the foreground suggests it is close up while the silhouette of the city looks much further away. • The bees breaking over into the margins suggest depth. The word "OUR" overlaps the background image creating depth. • The varying sizes of the bees in the layout suggest near and distant. • The flow text getting bigger appears to come toward the reader. • The paler tones of the smaller flow text make it appear further away. *Any three of the above.*	3
	(iv)	• The target market will be travelling somewhere when reading it and may not have time to read lots of detail. • A short slogan is more memorable than a paragraph of text. • A powerful Image has more immediate impact than lots of text. • The poster includes a link to more information. *Any two of the above.*	2
	(v)	For a maximum of two marks: Text edit – add a white outline to the letters/alter the size of words in the slogan (either for 1 mark). Justification – Sharpens up the text enabling it to stand out and be legible on a busy background/creates the impression of distance (depth) and adds to the visual impact (any one for 1 mark). **OR** Text edit – flow text along a path/ reverse text/add a drop shadow to 'OUR' (any one for 1 mark). Justification – adds movement that mimics the flight of a bee and adds visual interest/makes the slogan legible against a darker backdrop/adds emphasis to the key word (any one for 1 mark).	2

HIGHER FOR CfE
GRAPHIC COMMUNICATION
MODEL PAPER 2

Question		Comments	Marks
1	(i)	• Create a circle of DIA8mm. • Create a centre point from circle 156mm (radius of base sketch, minus the radius of circle). • Use revolve command @ 270degrees.	3
	(ii)	• Creating a path with the same dimensions as the hook (1 mark). • Create a profile of DIA8mm (1 mark). • Use 'Extrude along a path' (1 mark).	3
	(iii)	• Create a circle of DIA 70mm. • Create an offset workplane 60mm away. • Create a square of 55 mm on the 60mm offset workplane. • Create another workplane, offset 120mm from the first. • Create a circle of DIA 70mm on the 120mm offset workplane. • Loft the profiles. • Use the shell command @1.5mm, removing top face.	7

(iv)   7

40

39

10

Sketch the profile of half the candle holder. Constrain as shown
1 mark

Revolve the profile   1 mark
360°

Create a new sketch on the same workplane as the previous profile.
Draw a rectangle 10mm by 1mm
1 mark

Extrude 42mm to create a lip
1 mark

10

42

R5   Ø6

45

10

Create a new sketch on the lip and draw the profile above
1 mark

Extrude 1mm
1 mark

Circular Array the feature and repeat it once, 180 degrees from the first
1 mark

Question		Comments	Marks
2	(i)	Either of the answers shown below: Chain line cutting plane in the correct position AND arrows in correct direction. (1 mark) Inclusion of A-A label AND with thick ends. (1 mark)	2

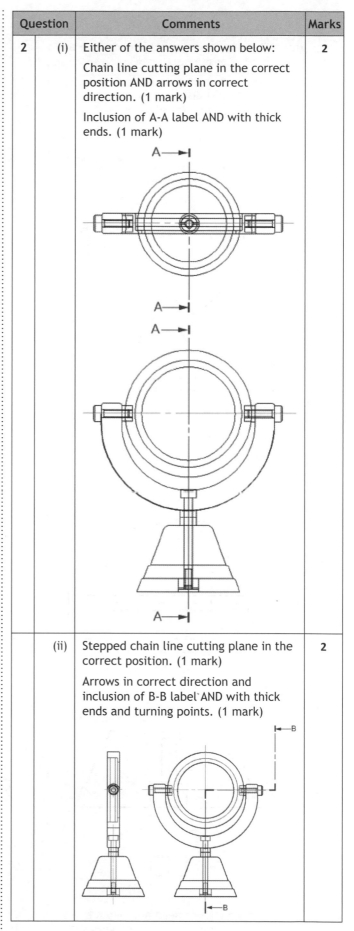

A⟶

A⟶
A⟶

A⟶

	(ii)	Stepped chain line cutting plane in the correct position. (1 mark) Arrows in correct direction and inclusion of B-B label AND with thick ends and turning points. (1 mark)	2

⊢—B

⊢—B

Question		Comments	Marks
	(iii)	Stepped chain line cutting plane in the correct position. (1 mark) Arrows in correct direction & Inclusion of C-C label AND with thick ends and turning points. (1 mark) 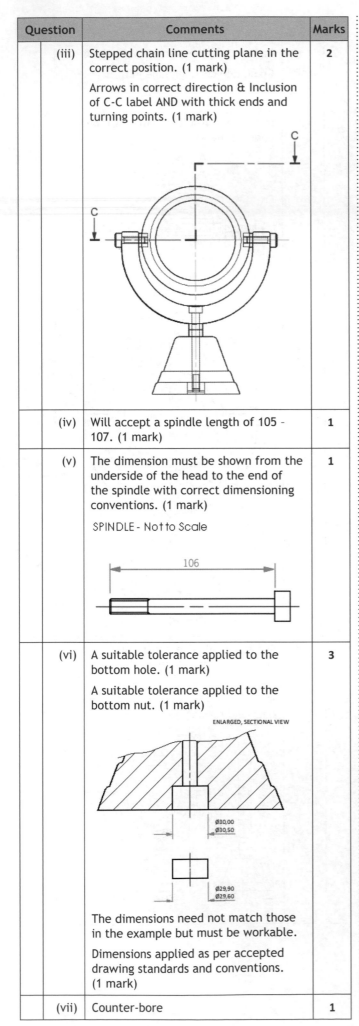	2
	(iv)	Will accept a spindle length of 105 – 107. (1 mark)	1
	(v)	The dimension must be shown from the underside of the head to the end of the spindle with correct dimensioning conventions. (1 mark) SPINDLE - Not to Scale 106	1
	(vi)	A suitable tolerance applied to the bottom hole. (1 mark) A suitable tolerance applied to the bottom nut. (1 mark) ENLARGED, SECTIONAL VIEW Ø30,00 Ø30,50 Ø29,90 Ø29,60 The dimensions need not match those in the example but must be workable. Dimensions applied as per accepted drawing standards and conventions. (1 mark)	3
	(vii)	Counter-bore	1

Question		Comments	Marks
	(viii)	Functional purpose: To enable the nut to be fitted without requiring feet to balance it OR to enable the nut to be fitted without loss of stability. (1 mark for either) Cosmetic purpose: To conceal the bottom nut. (1 mark)	2
	(ix)	The cross-hatched areas are part of the same component.	1
	(x)	It means that knurling (diamond) is to be added to the bolt during manufacture.	1
3	(i)	Layout 1 is an asymmetric layout. (1 mark) The off-centre focal point makes use of the rule of thirds to give the model impact. This layout leaves ample space for the body text to the left of the model. (Any one for 1 mark.) Layout 2 is a symmetrical layout, with the focal point in the centre. (1 mark) The body text has been squeezed into two areas either side of the centre. (1 mark)	4
	(ii)	Vertical and horizontal, black and white **or** light and dark (but not both), near and far (foreground and background), large and small font sizes, rectangular shapes and cropped figure. *Any two at 1 mark each.*	3
	(iii)	Transparencies are used to make the fill see through and a graded fill to change the tone along the fills. (1 mark each) Will accept white lines added.	2
	(iv)	• To ensure the background colours do not dominate the layout. • To reduce printing costs. • To create a harmonious colour scheme. • To ensure the model and his outfit is the dominant item in the layout. • To emphasise tonal contrast. • Will accept to create a sophisticated/retro or stylish look. *Any one of the above.*	1
	(v)	• It can help make the positioning of items easier. • The snap to grid feature can be activated to make positioning more accurate and quick. • It can help improve alignment of items. • It can be set to a size that suits the work being prepared. *Any two of the above.*	2

Question		Comments	Marks
	(vi)	Crop marks to show where the oversized paper is to be trimmed after printing.	1
	(vii)	Registration mark to show that the printing colours (or plates) are lined up correctly.	1
	(viii)	• This is the bleed area which is required when an item goes right to the edge of the finished page. • This bleed margin is set in the publication set up. • The bleed margin is trimmed off after printing. *Any two of the above.*	2
	(ix)	By using re-cycled paper and vegetable based (or environmentally approved) inks. It is also easier to separate vegetable inks from paper when the paper is being re-cycled.	1
	(x)	The images with the lowest resolution will be used in the online catalogue to enable customers to browse through many images quickly. (1 mark) The hi-resolution images will enable shoppers to view the clothes they have selected in high quality. (1 mark)	2
	(xi)	To prevent the theft of these images by competitors.	1
4	(i)	It does not rely on the reader having access to a tablet computer or internet connection. The magazine can be displayed in places where the target market is likely to buy it. Consumers are more prepared to pay for a physical copy of a magazine, rather than just digital content. Hard copy items are less likely to be illegally copied and distributed online.	2
	(ii)	The magazine will appeal to a broader range of people as it will have contributions from different countries and cultures. The publisher can recruit journalists from wider (global) selection as they do not have to come into an office to write for the publication. The publisher may not have face-to-face contact with journalists and this may make it difficult to manage production. Journalists have to email articles and images to the publisher – the journalist may not take images of sufficiently good quality. Files may be too large to email easily.	2
	(iii)	The magazine will appear larger and better value for money because of the number of pages with advertisements. The magazine can layout articles that may relate to particular advertisements.	2

Question		Comments	Marks
	(iv)	The magazine will appear larger and better value for money because of the number of pages with advertisements. The magazine can layout articles that may relate to particular advertisements.	2
5	(i)	Introduce a sub-heading under the title. (1 mark) Introduce a pull-quote. (1 mark)	2
	(ii)	• Add a drop shadow behind the image. • Crop the background away. • Rotate the image slightly. • Bleed the image off the page. • Place the image out-with the structure of the layout (a floating item). Wrap text around the image. • Place the image in white space. *Any three of the above.*	3
	(iii)	• Include a drop cap to the start of the body text. • Introduce paragraph breaks to break up the large block of text. Introduce a hanging indent at the start of the body text. • Introduce smaller raised caps at the start of each new paragraph. • Increase the leading a little. *Any two of the above.*	2

HIGHER FOR CfE GRAPHIC COMMUNICATION MODEL PAPER 3

Question		Comments	Marks
1	(i)	The different parts of the CAD model could be tested (1 mark) using FEA (1 mark). The different parts of the CAD model could be manufactured (1 mark) using CADCAM (1 mark) to create production drawing (1 mark).	4
	(ii)	• Create a path as shown in the elevation. • Create a circle of DIA 6mm. • Extrude along a path.	3
	(iii)	Draw a rectangle 4mm high, with the sides constrained to a centre axis, like above. Revolve the profile round the centre axis **1 mark** For the inne grips, draw DIA 2mm circles on a Pitch Circle Diameter of 12mm. **1 mark** Use the TANGENCY command to join them. Trim the curves to make the ridges as shown. **1 mark** Extrude these ridges 1mm **1 mark** Draw a DIA 2mm circle on the outside edge of the dial – with the centre on the edge. Polar Array this circle for 10 copies. **1 mark** Extrude and subtract this circle from the dial to create the grip. **1 mark**	6
	(iv)	• Create a profile of DIA 1mm. • Create a centre line 4mm from centre of circle. • Use helix command. • Set pitch to 1.5mm.	3
2	(i)	152.75mm	1
	(ii)	151.25mm	1
	(iii)	Revolved sections shows the part is made from a solid bar.	1

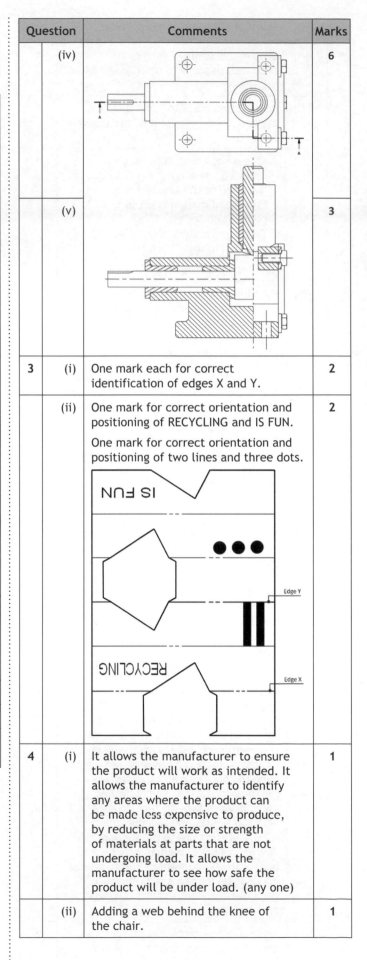

Question		Comments	Marks
	(iv)		6
	(v)		3
3	(i)	One mark each for correct identification of edges X and Y.	2
	(ii)	One mark for correct orientation and positioning of RECYCLING and IS FUN. One mark for correct orientation and positioning of two lines and three dots.	2
4	(i)	It allows the manufacturer to ensure the product will work as intended. It allows the manufacturer to identify any areas where the product can be made less expensive to produce, by reducing the size or strength of materials at parts that are not undergoing load. It allows the manufacturer to see how safe the product will be under load. (any one)	1
	(ii)	Adding a web behind the knee of the chair.	1

Question		Comments	Marks
	(iii)	• Can help design: testing 3D CAD models allow designers to refine ideas without using valuable materials. • Can help manufacturing: errors in the design can be detected prior to manufacture. Computer simulation can identify where materials can be made smaller or thinner, without making the product weaker. *Any one of the above.*	2
	(iv)	Predicting or training.	
5	(i)	Making a corporate presence or graphic design for a small screen that must also contain lots of information can be difficult. Different phones have different screen sizes and resolutions and this can affect the quality of the presentation – it can be difficult to plan a layout suitable for all models of phone. Touch screen phones use an 'on screen' keyboard – this can take up valuable space for a graphic design. The graphic design is a functional item and there can be little space or opportunity to showcase exciting designs.	2
	(ii)	Making a corporate presence or graphic design for a small screen that must also contain lots of information can be difficult. Different phones have different screen sizes and resolutions and this can affect the quality of the presentation – it can be difficult to plan a suitable layout. 1 mark for correctly identifying the range of information to be presented in a small area. 1 mark for describing size/resolution of screen and how this can impact upon the quality of the layout.	2
	(iii)	Using a pictograph, such as a flag representing the language of various countries.	1
	(iv)	There are security issues with customers using phones as a boarding pass – phones are targets for thieves. Phones may run out of battery and not be able to display the boarding pass. The screen may have a cracked screen and not be able to clearly display the boarding pass. The phone screen resolution may be too low to display the QR code clearly. The passenger may be less confident with phone technology and slow to load or display the phone boarding pass – slowing down the process of boarding the flight. *Any two of the above.*	2

Question		Comments	Marks
6	(i)	• The blue colour is introduced and is chosen to contrast with the red. • It is used throughout the article to unify the layout. • It is used in sub-heads to create visual rhythm in the layout. • It is used to emphasise the sub-heads, making the article easier to follow. *Any two of the above.*	2
	(ii)	Red is the most saturated colour in the layout and appears in the numbered circles. The red colour is intended to create emphasis (make the red circles stand out). The red colour creates contrast with the white background and the blue accent colour. Strong saturated colours appear in the vegetable images. This makes them stand out more and appear appetising or succulent. It also creates contrast with the green colours in the fruit images. *1 mark each for any two answers.*	2
	(iii)	• The image relating to a specific tip is placed close to the tip – this is called proximity. • Text wrap has been used to create even closer link between text and image. • The text is arranged in columns giving the layout a structure and making it easier to follow. • The blocks of text have been carefully aligned making the layout easier to follow. • The consistent use of colours in sub-heads creates a rhythm that flows and is easier to follow. • The body text is separated into bite-sized chunks that are easier to follow. *Any three of the above.*	3
	(iv)	It is the Cyan, Magenta, Yellow and Black (key colour) colour coding system. (1 mark) It is used to mix and describe colours for printing. The numbers determine the ratio of the mix of Cyan, Magenta, Yellow and Black used to achieve the blue in the layout. (Any one for 1 mark.)	2
	(v)	The colour appears to match the blue in the lunch bag. (1 mark) The designer probably sampled the colour on the bag with the colour picker tool and used the colour code to create the colour of the sub-heads. (1 mark)	2

Question		Comments	Marks
	(vi)	To create a less formal, less traditional or more visually interesting layout. (1 mark) These items are known as 'floating' items. They create visual contrast with the formal, structured appearance. More likely to appeal to a younger target market. (Any one for 1 mark.)	2
	(vii)	Arranging the three lines of text in a block. Using alignment over the three lines to maximise the block effect. Reducing the line spacing (leading) between the lines of text. Use of block caps increases mass and impact. Surrounding it with white space. *Any two at 1 mark each.*	2
	(viii)	Reducing the space between letters in a word/especially overlapping letters such as AV. (1 mark) It creates impact by increasing the 'slab' or 'block' effect of the text in the heading. (1 mark)	2
	(ix)	• There are legibility issues – a title has to be legible. • The choice of slender typefaces lacks the impact that is important in a title. • Slab fonts in the final one have more impact. • There are too many conflicting fonts (four in total) so it lacks continuity. • The typefaces don't complement each other as there are too many stylised typefaces. • The use of modern and script style fonts clash. • The chosen one has two sans serif fonts that look modern and work well together. *Any three of the above.*	3
	(x)	A typeface that has decorative flicks at the end of strokes.	1
	(xi)	A serif font adds contrast with the sans serif sub-heads and title fonts. (1 mark) A serif font may be easier to read because the serifs help the letters to flow together. (1 mark)	2
	(xii)	A PDF file requires less memory storage than a standard DTP file. A PDF file embeds the text and images and is much less likely to be altered accidentally. It is quicker to print a PDF file. It can be easier to send a PDF attached to an email. *Any one of the above.*	1

Question		Comments	Marks
	(xiii)	It bridges the gap in size between heading and body text. It creates another shape in the layout. It creates another visual component in the layout. It adds an often controversial teaser to draw the reader into the article. *Any one of the above.*	1

HIGHER FOR CfE GRAPHIC COMMUNICATION 2015

Question		Expected response	Max mark
1.	(a)	**Helix** • Describing a **profile** and **axis** (1 mark). • Describing feature command as **helix** (1 mark).	2
	(b)	**Pipe** • Describing **path**, with all **dimensions** (1 mark). • Describing **profile** with OD10 & ID7 (1 mark). • Feature command as **extrude along a path** (1 mark).	3
	(c)	**Nozzle** **Loft Method** • Loft command (1 Mark). • Loft from DIA30mm to DIA53 (1 Mark). • Offset to 241mm (1 mark). • Loft from DIA57mm to DIA58 offset to 13mm. (1 Mark). • Shell to 1mm and 3mm (1 Mark). • Hole DIA7mm on DIA30mm end (1 Mark). **Revolve Method** • Ensuring length of part 254mm (1 mark). • Ensuring diameters are DIA30mm DIA53 DIA57 DIA58mm (1 mark). • Ensuring part has a 1mm wall thickness and 3mm end wall thickness (1 mark). • Ensuring profile has correct pipe hole diameter 7mm (1 mark). • Creating a profile axis (1 mark). • Feature command as revolve (1 mark).	6
	(d)	**Wall Bracket** • Extruding L-shape bracket (1 mark). • Wall thickness of bracket is 10mm (1 mark). • Circular recess profile is between DIA114mm and 120mm and extrude (subtract) circular recess 5mm deep (1 mark). • Ensuring centre of hook is 32mm from the back of the wall bracket and positioned vertically (1 mark). • Ensuring hook is equal to or less than DIA10mm (1 mark). • Applying four screw holes to bracket (1 mark). • Height from bottom of recess to the bottom of the pin, size 376mm (1 mark).	7

Question		Expected response	Max mark
2.	(a)	**3P's** Figure 1 – **Promotional graphic** • realistic rendering of the building • shows how the completed building will fit in with its environment • promotion or advertising for the building Figure 2 – **Preliminary Graphic** • gives a sense of scale and/or form • no specific construction information can be gained • used to give a sense of how the concept may look Figure 3 – **Production Graphic** • shows how the building will be laid out • gives details of internal partitions and accommodation *One mark awarded per graphic.*	3
	(b)	**Scale** • size of item • size of paper • degree of detail required *One mark for each correct response.*	2
	(c)	**Cross Hatching** • describe different materials • describe different components • show parts that have been cut by the cutting plane *One mark for each correct statement.*	2
	(d)	**BS Symbols** Figure 4 – Window hinged at side Figure 5 – Existing tree to be removed Figure 6 – Contours *One mark awarded for each correct response.*	3
3.	(a)	**Advantages to the consumer** Responses should include; • a number of magazines/publications can be stored on a device • easy to zoom in or increase size of font • can be shared across a number of devices for the owner • sharing elements/videos/images on social media or email • instant links to websites (if needed) • can copy and paste content • no need to visit shop or wait for it to be delivered • videos can be embedded • can be read in the dark • available in different languages • better for the environment, with justification e.g. delivery costs, raw materials, printing costs • digital copies cost less than their paper versions to purchase • any other relevant answer *One mark for each correct response.*	2

Question		Expected response	Max mark
	(b)	**Advertising** Responses should include; • sharing elements/videos/images on social media or email • interactivity allows advertisers website to be accessed directly and instantly • potential purchasing of products is easier • live pricing on products • advantage of being able to add videos, animations, slideshows using the same amount of advertising space • any other relevant answer *One mark for each correct response.*	2
	(c)	**Distribution** Responses should include; • adaptability for different platforms/devices • target market limited due to affordability of devices • subscription services • Possible loss of jobs for print staff. Not offset by digital based employees. • digital rights management • internet access not always available • some potential users put off by digital media and prefer the printed version • any other relevant answer *One mark for each correct response.*	4
4.	(a)	**Scale** 1:20	1
	(b)	**Table Height** Max – 764mm Min – 758mm	2
	(c)	**Tolerances** 701,5 / 699,5 or +1,5 −0,5 / 700 +2,5 −1,5 / 60 or 62,5 / 58,5	2
	(d)	**BS threads**	2
	(e)	18mm	1
	(f)	20mm	1
	(g)	Parallel Dimensioning	1
	(h)	Part/local Section	1

Question			Expected response	Max mark
5.	(a)		**Connecting with the target audience:** • The use of a slender serif style which looks quite feminine. • The pink accent colour links to female target market. • Overlapping text creates a visually exciting effect. **Creating contrast** • several different typefaces, • use of reverse text (white text on black background) • different font sizes, • use of capital and lower case • use of serif/sans serif, • use of italics/standard, • staggered alignment, • use of two colours, • use of exaggerated quote marks • different line spacing creates visual interest *For full marks* *Either:* *1 from **target audience** and 3 from **creating contrast*** *2 from **target audience** and 2 from **creating contrast*** *3 from **target audience** and 1 from **creating contrast.***	4
	(b)	(i)	**Creating Unity** • Layering and overlapping one image over another. • The drop cap over the image creates a physical unity. • The use of the yellow accent colour in seven separate areas creates unity through colour. • The angle of the headline matching the angle of the drop cap and the highlighted area of the pull quote. • The graphic images are all on the same theme. *One mark for each correct response for 2 marks.*	2
		(ii)	**Proportion** • The use of a large dominant image on the left hand page leads the eye to the article and its' theme. • The size of the title also draws the reader to the article. • The drop cap's proportion leads the reader to the start of the body text. • The change in proportion of the three graphics on the right hand page creates interest and breaks from conformity. *One mark for each correct response for 2 marks.*	2

Question		Expected response	Max mark
	(c)	**Shape** • The column grid structure is rectangular in fact it is almost square. This creates a safe, formal look. • The green circle and the thin circles and add visual contrast against the rectangular structure. • The cropped photograph (or figurative outline) brings a strong irregular shape that suggests movement to the layout and contrasts with the very formal or rectilinear column structure. • The thin circles are not concentric and this creates a sense of movement and pattern that contrasts with the formality of the layout structure. • The full stops and circles used in the layout create rhythm through repetition. *Any three correct responses at one mark each.*	3
6.	(a)	**Colour** **Version 1:** • Too many colours that conflict or contrast with each other. • There is no unifying colour. • There is no accent colour tying the layout together. • Colour used to separate the areas. • Choice of bright colours doesn't suit the target market of 18–28. **Version 2:** • Uses harmonising tones of blue that create unity. • The red headings and sub-heads with the blue create visual interest and unity. • The red text is advancing and stands out. *Any one correct response from each version.*	2

Question		Expected response	Max mark
	(b)	**Alignment** **Version 1:** • The whole document is centre aligned. • The headline is centre aligned along with the 2013. • The rule is aligned with the column structure. • The sub heads are in alignment within their coloured boxes. • The sub-heads are in alignment with the graphics. • The body text columns are in alignment with the graphics and the sub-heads. • It is a very formal layout. • The strong alignment creates a clear structure. that is easy to follow. • Fully justified text adds to the strong alignment. **Version 2:** • The headline and 2013 are centre aligned. • The drop caps are all in alignment with the top edge of the text columns. • The 'R&R on the farm' sub-head is aligned with the text column. • The 'Blastin' Merry' sub-head is aligned with the bottom of the graphic. • The white border is centre aligned. • The informal layout creates interest. *For full marks* *Either* *1 from **Version 1** and 3 from **Version 2*** *2 from **Version 1** and 2 from **Version 2*** *3 from **Version 1** and 1 from **Version 2***	4
	(c)	**Balance** **Version 1:** • Uses a symmetrical balance resulting in a very formal look. • Formal, symmetrical, structure not likely to appeal to the TM. **Version 2:** • Uses an asymmetric balance that creates a youthful feel or look. • It is more of a challenge to find your way around because of the angles and rotated sub-heads. • Asymmetric balance provides visual interest that will appeal to the TM. *Any one correct response from each version.*	2

Question		Expected response	Max mark
	(d)	**Texture** **Version 1:** • There is a lack of texture in the document. • It is texturally bland and may not appeal to the TM as much as V2. **Version 2:** • The lined paper effect. • The ink splash top right create visual interest and a course, home-made quality. Their inclusion is intended to appeal to a young TM. • The blurred nature of the ink splash. *Any one correct response from each version.*	2
	(e)	**Emphasis** **Version 1:** • Uses colour fills to emphasise the names of the festivals. • The layout is flat; there is no use of layering to push items forward and create depth other than the colour fills behind the subheads. • The headline is suitably large and gives emphasis. • The headline is colourful and gives emphasis. • The headline is curved and gives emphasis. **Version 2:** • The colour fills behind the sub-heads push the sub-heads forward. • The colour fills are rotated to create an angular effect that makes them more obvious. • Drop shadows behind the headline, and images create emphasis. • Drop caps emphasise the start of the body text making it easy to locate where to begin reading. • Contrasting heading font with white outline. *Any one correct response from each version.*	2

Acknowledgements

Permission has been sought from all relevant copyright holders and Hodder Gibson is grateful for the use of the following:

Joanna Zopoth-Lipiejko/Shutterstock.com (SQP page 10);
Alex James Bramwell/Shutterstock.com (SQP page 10);
Dudarev Mikhail/Shutterstock.com (SQP page 22);
pio3/Shutterstock.com (SQP page 22);
Monkey Business Images/Shutterstock.com (SQP page 22);
Warren Goldswain/Shutterstock.com (SQP page 22);
l i g h t p o e t/Shutterstock.com (SQP page 22);
Sergey Lavrentev/Shutterstock.com (SQP page 22);
archideaphoto/Shutterstock.com (SQP page 23);
Getty Images/Wavebreakmedia Ltd/Thinkstock (Model Paper 1 page 16);
FotoMaximum/iStock/Thinkstock (Model Paper 1 page 16);
Getty Images/PhotoObjects.net/Thinkstock (Model Paper 1 page 16);
Ase/Shutterstock.com (Model Paper 1 page 19);
YurkaImmortal/Shutterstock.com (Model Paper 1 page 19);
LilKar/Shutterstock.com (Model Paper 1 page 19);
Peter Waters/Shutterstock.com (Model Paper 1 page 19);
Vitalii Hulai/Shutterstock.com (Model Paper 1 page 19);
Nature Art/Shutterstock.com (Model Paper 1 page 19);
Alexandra Giese/Shutterstock.com (Model Paper 1 page 19);
Ysbrand Cosijn/Getty Images/iStock/Thinkstock (Model Paper 2 pages 14, 15 & 17);
Cover of MAKE Magazine © Maker Media, Inc (Model Paper 2 page 19);
hurricanehank/Shutterstock.com (Model Paper 2 page 20);
Aleksandra Gigowska/Shutterstock.com (Model Paper 3 pages 13 & 14);
Bufo/Shutterstock.com (Model Paper 3 pages 15 & 19);
Two images by Serg64/Shutterstock.com (Model Paper 3 pages 15 & 19);
Hal_P/Shutterstock.com (Model Paper 3 pages 15 & 19);
Vanatchanan/Shutterstock.com (Model Paper 3 pages 15 & 19);
Creativa Images/Shutterstock.com (Model Paper 3 pages 15 & 19);
Two images by Andresr/Shutterstock.com (Model Paper 3 pages 15 & 19);
Three images of the Glasgow Riverside Museum of Transport. Reproduced by permission of Zaha Hadid Architects (2015 page 8);
An extract from Cosmopolitan, September 2013. Interview by Elaine Lipworth & photograph by James White © Cosmopolitan Magazine UK (2015 page 18);
An extract from Extreme sports magazine. Design: danmackay.com.au (2015 page 19);
An extract from Vibe Magazine, May 5 2007. Article by Hillary Crosley & photo by Kaseem Black (2015 page 20);
Maxim Blinkov/Shutterstock.com (2015 Supplementary Sheet);
Dziurek/Shutterstock.com (2015 Supplementary Sheet);
Christian Bertrand/Shutterstock.com (2015 Supplementary Sheet);
melis/Shutterstock.com (2015 Supplementary Sheet).

Hodder Gibson would like to thank SQA for use of any past exam questions that may have been used in model papers, whether amended or in original form.